Not for Bread Alone

Not for

Foreword by Ossie Davis

Bread Alone

A MEMOIR

by **Moe Foner**

with Dan North

Cornell University Press *Ithaca and London*

First published 2002 by Cornell University Press

Printed in the United States of America

Library of Congress Cataloging-in-Publication Data

Foner, Moe, 1915–
    Not for bread alone : a memoir / by Moe Foner ; with Dan North ; foreword by Ossie Davis.
        p. cm.
Includes bibliographical references and index.
    ISBN 0-8014-4061-0 (acid-free paper)
    1. Foner, Moe, 1915–   2. Labor leaders—New York (State)—Biography.
3. Hospitals—Staff—Labor unions—New York (State)—History.   I.
North, Dan.   II. Title.
    RA971.35 .F66 2002
    331.88'092—dc21   2002005100

Cornell University Press strives to use environmentally responsible suppliers and materials to the fullest extent possible in the publishing of its books. Such materials include vegetable-based, low-VOC inks and acid-free papers that are recycled, totally chlorine-free, or partly composed of nonwood fibers. For further information, visit our website at www.cornellpress.cornell.edu

Cloth printing   10 9 8 7 6 5 4 3 2 1

Contents

Foreword

by Ossie Davis

Somewhere just South of the Center of our
Deepest Affection, There He Abides,
Our Very Own Hero of Labor: Moe Foner

ON MAY 17, 1954, the Supreme Court of the United States ended segregation with the *Brown v. Board of Education* decision. The infamous *Plessy v. Ferguson* precedent was dead. The separate-but-equal standard was horrendous—sometimes deadly, based on the assumption that black folks were inherently inferior to white folks. We never accepted the premise, but segregation was the only lifestyle we knew. The decision was a gift, not only to us but to all Americans, a reward for years of valiant struggle. But it didn't come with instructions.

Everybody knew that something momentous had occurred. It said flat out that many laws and practices by which we Americans conducted our daily race relations were unconstitutional. That was a big relief, something we had argued for and struggled to get since 1896. But now that we had it, how did we make it work? Obviously some serious changes had to be made. But who was to make these changes and when? In the black community there was much waiting around to see how the rest of America, the white South in particular, would respond to what the Court had said.

The answer, even from Congress, was not encouraging, expressing an almost total opposition to what the Court had ruled.

It wasn't until August 1955 and the murder of Emmett Till, a 15-year-old black boy from Money, Mississippi, that things began to change. When we looked down on the mangled and viciously beaten body of Emmett, traveling around the country in his open coffin, black folks began to be pulled into the struggle, compelled to speak and to act for ourselves. In December, Rosa Parks provided the spark when she refused to give up her seat on a bus in Montgomery, Alabama. A boycott of the bus line was called for, and we became a Movement, as Martin Luther King, Jr., called us all into battle. It was at that time that Ruby Dee and I first met Moe Foner and Local 1199, then a small union of largely white male drugstore workers from New York, and through them found our rightful place in the grassroots line of the march.

Ruby and I had begun our civil rights activism by acting in a benefit performance of a play called *Anna Lucasta* in 1946 to raise money for the families of two soldiers killed by the Klan in Monroe, Georgia. After that, like many other performers on Broadway and in Hollywood, black and white, we demonstrated, picketed, and rallied—anything to raise consciousness and funds, mostly for the NAACP and the Urban League. But our activism was mostly scattershot and happenstance. It was at Local 1199 under the tutelage of Moe Foner that we finally found the focus and began to fulfill in the deepest, most personal way our commitment to the struggle, rendering our most conspicuous service to the cause.

Moe was looking for performers for the union's "Negro History Week," and Madeline Gilford suggested Ruby Dee and me; we happened to be working nearby in an off-Broadway production of *The World of Sholom Aleichem*. Moe sent for us and offered us a minimal fee to come to 1199 and perform for the membership. Ruby and I had routinely appeared in such programs at a black church, school, or college each February, offering readings from the works of Frederick Douglass, Phillis Wheatley, Paul Laurence Dunbar, and Langston Hughes. So we jumped at the chance.

But Moe from the start was looking for something more than a mere recitation of poems and speeches from the past. What about the present, he asked me and Ruby, something current, something directly connected to the struggle for civil rights just beginning to command the country's attention? Ruby and I became excited. Why not an original piece, I replied, a little drama on what was happening in the daily headlines swirling around us, which we would stage for the membership by standing up and reading into a microphone, living newspaper–style? I was a writer as well as an actor, so why not?

Our first collaboration was a piece we called "The People of Clarendon County," based on one of the cases that had led to the 1954 Supreme Court decision. It told of how the people of Clarendon County, under the leadership of the Reverend Joseph Armstrong De Laine, sued the state of South Carolina for better schools for their children, and how Judge J. Waties Waring suggested they take their case all the way up to the Supreme Court, where it was filed with four other suits attacking school segregation.

We hired one other actor, William Marshall, to play the role of the Reverend De Laine, and Ruby and I did all the other parts. We performed it in front of the membership of Local 1199 and received a standing ovation. And that was how Ruby and Ossie and Moe formed our own little collective, a production unit at 1199.

For the next four or five years, the three of us would huddle together in February in Moe's office and repeat the creative process, dramatizing whatever we found in the headlines that pertained to the burgeoning struggle for civil rights, which was finally grabbing the attention of Americans and of the world. We wrote, staged, directed, and produced such presentations as *What Can You Say to Mississippi?*, about the death of Emmett Till; *Montgomery Footprints*, about the Montgomery bus boycott; and *Martin Luther King, Jr.*, for which we hired Will Geer, another distinguished actor. Some of the other performers we employed for subsequent shows were Lena Horne, Ricardo Montalban, Pete Seeger, Beah Richards, Maya Angelou, John Randolph, and Sara Cunningham.

These were heady, productive, artistically fulfilling years for Ruby and me and for Moe, who was always looking for new ways to bring culture and art to the workers, not only at the union hall but also at the workplace. One of the most exciting of Moe's new projects was Bread and Roses, the cultural project he founded in 1978, and *Take Care*, a Bread and Roses musical revue based on the life of hospital workers, which Ruby and I helped create.

So many things have changed since we first met Moe Foner, and for good or bad they have been changed forever. When we were young we thought of "labor" as physical, a thing you did with your body, your legs, your hands, where the use of muscle and movement was mandatory. Sometimes pencil and paper, and even a typewriter, were involved. And at the end of the day there was something new in the world that had your mark on it: a product, a commodity, a work that you could be proud of and call your own even if it did belong to the factory or to the farm or to the boss in the marketplace. Life consisted in many ways of work to be done—a road to be paved, a house to be built, a brick to be laid, a nail to be hammered and a home created; cotton to be picked, acres to be planted, and harvests to be reaped and stacked and stored; a meal to be prepared, a floor to be mopped, socks to be mended, dirty laundry to be washed, and children to be raised; students to be taught, sermons to be preached, bodies to be buried in coffins fashioned by grief as well as handicraft, and a baby to give birth to. A man or woman was defined by what he or she did and the way he or she did it.

These activities established who we were and made us authentic and real. Labor anchored us, defined us, and slowly made us into human beings, related to the earth and all its habits. And for Moe Foner, chief among these habits was art, the highest form of labor. Moe brought art to the workers, enriching their lives.

A better ending would be if we could come together—the old collective: Ruby, Ossie, and Moe—just one more time. Sitting around the table in his office getting down to business. What will be our subject for Negro History Week? How stands the cause of workers in the new world order? What champion and martyr best exemplifies the struggle to humanize technology and get all the workers of the world a better contract in the global market? We'd brainstorm like we did in the old days and then, to break the impasse: Why not do the life of Moe himself, just the short version of course. I could write it and direct it and maybe play the part of Martin Luther King, Jr. Ruby could play the part of Moe's wife Anne (a play about Moe would be full of Anne or it wouldn't work) and Mrs. Roosevelt. Then maybe we could get Dennis Rivera, president of 1199, now a 210,000–member union, to play the part of Moe, except that Dennis is so quiet and polite—not exactly the Moe that we remember.

Or maybe Moe's brother Henry. Except that Henry would insist on singing all the lines.

Suddenly, the man I would present no longer stands beside me. Moe. Moe Foner, to whom I could always turn for guidance and good advice, is dead. And what began as prologue is now obituary. I seek the proper way to confront this harsh transition, but words, which are my gift, begin to falter; the enormity of our loss confounds the tongue. If Moe were here, as Moe has always been whenever I needed his strength, I'd turn to him, as many times I have, to seek the answer to my final question: Moe, is this the proper way to say good-bye?

Acknowledgments

IN 1984 BOB MASTER, then my co-worker at Local 342 of the Amalgamated Meatcutters Union, suggested that we preserve some of my experiences on tape. Our talks, which concluded in 1986, became a part of the Columbia University Oral History Project. At that time, a memoir was the furthest thing from my mind. But in 2000, when the Columbia Project posted my oral history on its website, the project's director, Mary Marshall Clark, suggested that I do a memoir. And so began what turned out to be both a personal and a collective project. Many people have helped me tell my story.

I owe special thanks to the following people for their invaluable support:

Dan North brought Columbia's oral history interviews up to date and then, using the 991-page oral history as his major source, turned all that raw material into a manageable and readable book. In doing so, Dan called on knowledge acquired in his work since 1968 as editor at *1199 News*. He has been both a thoughtful collaborator and a valuable friend.

My brother Henry has been a devoted supporter throughout the project. He has read every chapter, corrected my mistakes, and reminded me of events I had forgotten. Betsy Wade, who recently ended her long and distinguished career at the *New York Times*, took time out from her vacation to go over the whole manuscript and give me the benefit of her professional expertise and wisdom. Bernie Mazel responded to my almost daily phone calls with insightful advice. Milton Glaser, the renowned illustrator, contributed his artistic talent, and Charlotte Stimpson, Milton's assistant, and Katja Maas, graphic designer on his staff, smoothed the way. I am indebted to all for their unstinting help.

My wife, Anne, and daughters, Nancy and Peggy, provided assistance in a category all its own. As only family members can do, they read with a critical eye and did not hold back with honest opinions. But they also were supportive and reassuring.

I am grateful to so many others who read at least some of the chapters, encouraged me, and made important suggestions. I am fortunate to have had such insightful readers. These included old and new friends such as Nathaniel Brooks (who also enlisted the reaction of long-time union activist Tom Deary), Perry Bruskin, David Cohen, George Kirschner (who also grew up in Williamsburg), Tara Levy, Ella Mazel, Terry Sadin, and Victor Teich. Insightful readings also came from my nephew, Eric Foner; my brother-in-law, Mark Berman; my son-in-law, Peter Swerdloff; and my granddaughter, Alexis Swerdloff.

Colleagues at 1199 and elsewhere in the Service Employees International Union (SEIU) whose comments were helpful included Dennis Rivera, president of New York's Health and Human Service Union, 1199/SEIU, who wrote me from prison in Puerto Rico, where he was serving 30 days for peacefully protesting the U.S. Navy's bombing of the Puerto Rican island of Vieques; Kay Anderson, Rivera's executive assistant; Jesse Olson, former 1199 executive vice president who checked facts about 1199 history; Eleanor Tilson, executive director of the 1199 Benefit Fund; J. J. Johnson, editor of *1199 News*; Larry Fox, a former officer of 1199/New England; Michael Myerson, an 1199 communications consultant; and Nina Shapiro-Perl, director of SEIU's Greenhouse Project.

The members of the staff of the Bread and Roses Cultural Project whose help was invaluable included cultural director Esther Cohen, Rachel Burd, William Johnson, Margot Jones, Amanda Sapir, and Andrea Stupka (who helped shepherd the manuscript through various stages), Bonita Savage, Terry Sullivan, Rytva Tilson, and volunteer Ann Newman-Bacal.

Professional friends who were supportive include Gene Carroll, Paula Finn, Herbert Kohl, Linda Markstein, and Anne Sparanese. *1199 News* photographers Jim Tynan and Belinda Gallegos were enormously helpful in gathering photographs.

A number of individuals and foundations made it possible to distribute the book more widely to union members. My heartfelt gratitude to Ballen and Company, Robert Boehm, the Gerald & Thelma Estrin Living Trust, the Andrew Goodman Foundation, Lucille Perlman, the Louis M. Rabinowitz Foundation, Inc., Marcia Rabinowitz, the Samuel Rubin Foundation, Herman Warsh, and the Weissman Family Foundation.

Allee Johnson, who helps care for me at home, has been of invaluable assistance in making it possible for me to work here.

It has been a pleasure to work with the staff of Cornell University Press. I am grateful to Fran Benson, Priscilla Hurdle, Cathy Reinfelder, George Whipple, and all the others at Cornell who encouraged me and helped shepherd the book to publication.

This book is neither a scholarly work nor a history of 1199. I don't pretend to have answers for many of the issues raised here, nor was I a frontline participant in all of 1199's many achievements. What I have tried to do here is tell what I did and saw. In putting this story on paper I salute the 1199 members of today and yesterday who, in helping to build the good society, were the force behind most of the events described in this book.

Not for Bread Alone

1. Saturdays at the Palace

Growing Up in Brooklyn

M Y FATHER always stooped. He was bent over from long days of carrying seltzer bottles up four and five flights of tenement stairs. He was a seltzer man when I was a boy in Brooklyn, and he was always tired.

In my earliest memories of him, I'd be in the playground across the street from our apartment in Williamsburg, and I'd see him coming from work. It would be around half past seven in the evening. He'd have left his horse and delivery wagon at the stable and would be walking from South First Street, exhausted and still grimy from the day's work. He'd be bowed down, looking at the ground.

Abraham Foner was his name. We called him Papa. He was born in 1884 in Bielsk, in what was then Russia and now Poland. He came to this country at the age of fifteen with his parents and seven siblings. He was quiet, with a medium build and a pockmarked face. I don't recall a warm or close relationship with my father. He was quiet and always tired. But he did all the things a father in those days was supposed to do. We were no poorer than the rest of our neighbors, and we were never hungry. And he gave us the example of someone who worked hard all his life.

That was the main thing when I was growing up. Work. We were always working. I started young and even today, at eighty-six, I don't feel ready to stop. We hardly ever ate meals together because everyone—my father, my three brothers, and I—were always running off at different hours to school or a job. After he was a seltzer man, my father and a partner ran a garage for quite a few years, the St. Clair Garage at Pearl and Tillary Streets in downtown Brooklyn. The work was hard and the hours long. That and my father's constant smoking took a toll on his health, and he had to get out of the garage business. In his last years he delivered eggs to all our friends in Brooklyn to stay busy and have some income.

He had a hard life, my father. He didn't read books and wasn't particularly interested in culture, religion, or politics. He took his main satisfactions from things close to home. The main thing was family. He took deep pride in the achievement of his children, urging us to get an education and move up in the world, and then basking in our reflected glory whenever any of us met with success.

As the eldest of eight siblings, my father was looked up to with respect. Most of the family lived nearby. My father would preside over the brothers' weekly meetings, discussing family matters and the contributions made for the upkeep of their parents by the various brothers and sisters. I remember going to one of those meetings and watching my grandfather smoke, drink tea, and write letters to the Yiddish newspaper the *Forward*. The *Forward*'s letters section was called the *Bintel Brief* (Bundle of Letters), and it would have all kinds of stories about immigrant hardships.

My father also played an important role in a fraternal organization, the *Bielsker Bruderlicher Unterstitzen Verein*, which was made up of people from his native region in Russia. He attended its meetings religiously and served on various committees.

My father had a sharp sense of humor. I guess you could call it wry. He was always twisting things into a joke. The family story goes that when my older identical twin brothers, Phil and Jack, were born in my parents' apartment, which was then on the Lower East Side, my father came home from work and found my mother in tears over the extra work the two babies presented.

"How am I going to take care of twins?" she cried. "One is enough."

Papa bent over to take his first look at Phil and Jack, who were sleeping on my parents' bed. He pointed and said:

"Don't worry, that one don't look so good."

Phil and Jack argued for years over whom he was pointing at. Phil died in 1994 and Jack in 1999, so I guess the question will never be settled.

My mother was the heart and soul of our home. Her maiden name was Mary Smith, and since she came from Poland we thought maybe the "Smith" was given to her by an immigration official when she arrived at Ellis Island. We never discussed with either parent the details of their courtship and marriage, but the continuing close relationship that my mother's Aunt Rose had with our family led me to believe there may have been an arranged marriage.

Mama was a housewife all her life. She had dark good looks and was generous, even-tempered, and respected by everybody. She had few political or intellectual interests, but she loved to listen to the radio. I remember her listening to *The Rise of the Goldbergs* and, every Saturday afternoon, the Metropolitan Opera. She was a terrible cook. I remember eating a lot of tuna sandwiches, chopped liver, and cottage cheese with sour cream as a boy. The highlight of the week was chicken on Friday night. But Mama was the one I could always talk to, and I felt I had a special relationship with her.

A sad thing about her life was that she wanted very much to learn to read and write but she never could, no matter how hard we tried to help her. In addition to Yiddish, she spoke English well, without an accent, and I'm sure it bothered her that her sons did well scholastically while she remained illiterate in both Yiddish and English.

When I was little, I'd read to her a few times a week. I'd sit by the window in the kitchen while she worked and read stories to her from *The Book of Knowledge*. This was a set of volumes like an encyclopedia, probably bought one volume at a time from a door-to-door salesman. They were the only books I remember my parents bringing into the house. I'd read her stories like "Dick Whittington's Cat," children's stories that we both enjoyed. Then she'd have me iron the family's handkerchiefs while she made My-T-Fine chocolate pudding for me. The pudding was a big event in itself. Those were our special times together.

The twins were born late in 1910. I was born on August 3, 1915, and our youngest brother, Henry, came along four years later. The

twins were a tough act to follow. They were not only brilliant, they
were popular. They were always at the top of their class academi-
cally—from P.S. 19 and Eastern District High School, where we all
went, to City College and then Columbia. They both became historians. Phil was well known for his many books on American labor
and black history, and Jack, in addition to his teaching and lecturing
career at Colby College and elsewhere, was the father of the historian Eric Foner. But that's another story.

Besides being top students, Phil and Jack were stars of the baseball team and members of one of the best high school debating
teams in the city. One of their debating opponents was Gus Tyler,
later an assistant to the president of the International Ladies Garment Workers Union and still a journalist of distinction. Phil and
Jack also had a band, they were in school dramatics, and they were
officers of the General Organization, the student government.

Our house at 310 South Third Street was a center for all kinds of
people. The baseball team would be there, the band would be re-
hearsing, and later on, when we got older, there would be talk about
politics and other intellectual matters. The place was like a restaurant. My mother served meals at all times, and my father, when he
was home, was happy to see all the activity.

Almost everybody who came was Jewish. It was a big deal when
my brothers brought home their team's pitcher, Serge Grinkovich.
He was Russian but not a Jew. It was as if a precedent was shattered, like he might have horns. My parents didn't know what to do.
When he left, everyone was quiet for a minute. Then my father said,
"Hey, he wasn't so bad after all." It broke the tension and we all
laughed.

It may be that Phil and Jack gave me a sense of inadequacy by
comparison. On the first day of school every September, the teacher
would look at me and say, "Are you—." And I'd interrupt before
they could say "Phil and Jack's brother" and say "Yes." And they'd
expect great things from me that I couldn't deliver. I was an average
student at best. I sat in the back of the room and my eyesight was
terrible. I couldn't see what was written on the blackboard, but I
thought only sissies wore glasses. I did very little homework and I
practically lived on the playground.

My parents expected us to do well in school, and I remember the embarrassment I felt on spring nights when the twins and their friends would be out on the street doing algebra problems with chalk on the pavement. To me it meant nothing, and I felt not good enough and left out.

I did like to read, though. There was the Williamsburg Library, and a bookstore where you could get western novels that you could trade in every week, and the candy store where you bought Nick Carter or Frank and Dick Merriwell paperbacks. We all did a lot of reading, and adventure stories like these seemed to float in and out of our hands and move around the neighborhood. Not great literature.

Although I absorbed from my brothers the idea of debating, my idea of subject matter was different from theirs. When my sandlot baseball team, the Eagles, met at the neighborhood YMHA, I introduced the idea of a debate, laying out this question: "Resolved, that the Pittsburgh Pirates will win the 1925 World Series."

I played softball, pitched on the Eagles, and was captain of the Eastern District basketball team. I wasn't a great basketball player, but I was tall for my age and I was steady. When it came time to go to college I chose Brooklyn College because I knew I was too slow for Coach Nat Holman's fast-break style at City College of New York. My claim to fame is that our team played in the first college basketball game at the old Madison Square Garden on 50th Street. I couldn't believe it when I went to the foul line and the public address system boomed out my name. I almost plotzed on the spot. I can't remember if I made the foul shot or not. Another brush with greatness came when one of my Brooklyn College teammates—Marius Russo—went on to become an outstanding pitcher for the New York Yankees. However, after a couple of years sitting on the bench at Brooklyn College, I realized my future lay other than in athletics.

My parents weren't particularly religious, although we did observe major holidays. I remember the four of us standing in the synagogue on Marcy Avenue next to my father during the Yom Kippur services. That holiday often falls at the same time as the World Series, so we'd take turns running outside for the score while my father's head bobbed up and down over his prayer book.

I went to Hebrew school for a while, mostly to socialize. I had my bar mitzvah like other boys, but only because it was expected of me. Our neighborhood was so Jewish that it wasn't until we were practically adults that we were really aware of the larger culture around us. Once in a while Italian and Polish kids from Greenpoint would come through in groups of four or five and beat you up if they found you on the street. They came with stockings with cinders in them, and they really let you have it. This never happened to me or my brothers, though. It happened usually on Halloween night, and my parents would keep us indoors then.

While I used the playground and basketball to separate myself from no-win competition with my older brothers, my younger brother Henry was set apart because he suffered from rickets as a child and one of his legs was shorter than the other (or longer, as Henry said, depending on your point of view). Henry had to wear special shoes and was limited in sports. He was a very able student, became a teacher, and then had a long career as a leader in the Furriers Union. During my years as a basketball player, Henry went to all the games. He became the manager of the high school team. One of the players was Arnold "Red" Auerbach, who later broke all records as the coach of the fabled Boston Celtics. Henry claims one of his duties as manager was to help Auerbach pass algebra so he could remain eligible to play.

Sports were big in our neighborhood, and lots of Jews were athletes. Auerbach was just one of many kids we knew who went on to play in college and the pros. We used to argue about whether certain ballplayers were Jewish. Baseball players at that time were mostly farm boys, and when the Giants had a player named Andy Cohen, we were really proud.

It was always a big deal when we took the trolley to Ebbets Field and sat in the bleachers to watch the Dodgers play. They had a lousy team, always near the cellar, but some of the players like the pitcher Dazzy Vance and the left fielder Zach Wheat were our heroes. Sometimes at the end of the game we'd sneak onto the field through the dugout. That was like hallowed ground, like walking through Gettysburg.

Sometime in summer, my mother would send us out to Flushing

for a month in the country with her large and assertive Aunt Rose (Tante Rosie, or TR, as our boyhood friend Sammy Levenson, the future comedian, used to call her in a sly reference to former President Theodore Roosevelt). Flushing was nothing but goats and cows and farms back then. We took the elevated train to Jamaica, the 164th Street trolley, and then walked the rest of the way to the general store owned by Tante Rosie and Uncle Hersch (his real name was Harris Jeffer). The chickens they kept in the basement were later the basis for my father's egg route. Henry and I played cowboys and Indians out there.

Tante Rosie was always raising funds for the Jewish Home for Incurables (now known as the Hospital for Chronic Diseases). She once sold Sammy Levenson a batch of raffle tickets. After he paid he took a closer look.

"TR," he said, "these raffles were drawn last month!"

"That's all right," she replied smoothly. "You wouldn't have won anyway."

Williamsburg was a small town in a big city back then. It was a tightly knit community where people knew their neighbors. Some of the boys we grew up with became famous athletes or gangsters or surgeons or millionaire businessmen, but when we were little we all roasted potatoes out in the street together and played basketball in the playground or at the Y. Mothers would interrupt our street games with instructions to go to the store. They'd drop down coins and then lower a rope to hoist up the apples or bread we'd bought. The women washed clothes in the kitchen tub and shouted to each other across the back courtyard as they hung the wash out to dry on clotheslines. We lived close together. Henry and I slept in our parents' bedroom, and the twins shared the other bedroom. Neighbors handed around the Sunday papers to share the comics. We also got the *Forward*. Sometimes, after scrubbing the floor on her hands and knees, my mother spread newspapers to dry it. I liked to read the spread papers. Once, reading the *Forward* rotogravure that way, I saw a photo of Phil and Jack. They'd graduated high school at the top of their class.

In the summer one of the big things was to go to Coney Island. Mama would be the schlepper. She'd spend the day before preparing food, and then she'd schlep two big bags along the boardwalk, and Henry and I and our neighbor Frankie Herbst would run around to the Washington Baths Annex to change and swim in the pool. My mother wouldn't put on a bathing suit. She'd sit in the hot sun on the beach in her street clothes and wait. We were never there when we were supposed to be, and she'd send a cop to look for us. When we were older we'd walk around singing all the latest songs from the song sheets and memorizing the lyrics. And in the ocean we'd swim "rocks"—from rock jetty to rock jetty. Each rock was two blocks, a long distance, and we used to swim ten to twenty rocks without stopping. We were young. At that time, we mostly hung around with guys. Very few girls, they were separate. You looked at them and sometimes talked with them, but not very often. That came later.

Frank Herbst and I remained friends until he died of cancer in 1979. He was in real estate, and in the 1970s, as a volunteer, helped Local 1199 put together the deal that enabled us to build the 1199 Plaza housing development along the East River between 107th and 111th Streets in Manhattan.

When I was in my late teens we moved to Boro Park, also in Brooklyn. (The Herbsts moved there at the same time.) Later, my parents moved in with Tante Rosie. My father, who never liked Tante Rosie, hated that arrangement.

Although my father and mother did all the things they were expected to do as parents, I don't remember a very loving relationship between them. For one thing, I don't remember them being together very much.

My father died in 1959 after a car accident. He was seventy-four. He got lost one night and drove into the channel in Far Rockaway.

He may have been distant, but Papa was dedicated to our success. When we were busy teenagers with jobs and extracurricular activities, he used most of his spare time driving us around. Our achievements provided meaning to his life.

Publication in 1946 of my brother Phil's book on Thomas Paine coincided with my brother Henry's return home from the Army. Papa met Henry at Penn Station and almost his first words were:

"Have you heard about Phil's new book?"

"Is it good?" Henry asked.

"Good?" snorted my father. "It's thirteen hundred pages!"

My mother had a fatal stroke in 1967. When she died in a nursing home in Long Beach, there was this big debate outside on the street. Tante Rosie's sons had competing funeral parlors. Both wanted the job, they said, not for the business but for the honor. After lots of yelling and finger-pointing, we decided that Irwin would get the service and Norman could have the burial.

One reason we survived through my early years and through the Depression of the 1930s was that we were always working, and, until each brother got married and moved out, we all put our earnings into the household money. My older brothers worked in the post office throughout college. Before that they had a job for Brooklyn Edison. We lived in the last section of Brooklyn where the electric streetlights were not on an automatic switch, and their job was to turn each streetlight off with a key early each morning and turn them back on in the early evening. You had to walk four or five miles, but you got paid seven dollars a week, which was good money. I inherited the morning half of that job when Phil and Jack were in college. Sort of like hand-me-down clothing. But we had this problem. The supervisor was a mean bastard, and my brothers were sure he'd say I was too young. So they never told him. They taught me the route and told me I had to start so early that the supervisor would never see me. It worked. So I was getting up long before daylight to turn off the streetlights, going to school, and afterward practicing and playing basketball.

Brooklyn Edison wasn't my first job. For a while in my early teens I was in charge of the scoreboard on Broadway near the Brooklyn side of the Williamsburg Bridge. There was a pool hall with a news ticker and a swinging window with a blackboard on it. You chalked the Dodger scores on the blackboard and then swung the window around so the bystanders outside could see it. Large crowds stood below. Not so many people had radios back then, and they were willing to stand and wait until each inning was over to get the score. It was like watching grass grow, or ice melt.

Maybe I got my start in show biz there in a small way. You could influence the crowd by the way you gave them the score. For instance, if the Dodgers scored five runs in the top of the inning and the Braves scored two runs in the bottom of the inning, I'd reverse the order and give the Braves' two runs first. The crowd would groan. I'd wait a moment to tease them, and then give them the Dodgers' five runs. They'd go wild. I was just a kid, but I already liked having inside information and using it to get the result I wanted.

Another early job I had was selling buttons and pennants at weekend football games at Yankee Stadium or the Polo Grounds. You'd go in the morning to the outlet on Park Row in lower Manhattan. Maybe you'd buy pennants at twenty cents each and sell them for seventy-five cents. It took me a long time to learn that you had to lower the price as the afternoon wore on if you wanted to sell everything you'd bought.

My first real job was at Gimbels Department Store in Manhattan. I was fourteen or fifteen when I went with Benny Glick, who lived in my building, to the Gimbels employment office. We only halfway wanted a job, but we wanted to show our parents we were looking. Were we shocked when they hired us as stockboys. My job for the next two years was hanging things up and putting on price tags weekdays from four to eight and all day Saturdays. I got ten dollars a week. We'd take the train over the Williamsburg Bridge to 34th Street. But the parameters at home were tight. You just went to work and came back. You didn't wander off. And you had to get home in a hurry because your mother would hold food for you. It wouldn't occur to us to waste money by eating out, and we'd be hungry.

Times like those are probably why I eat the way I do. I eat very fast and I never stop to really enjoy food. When I went to elementary school, I lived across the street and I used to run home for lunch. In high school, I ran home about eight blocks, grabbed a hard-boiled egg or something, and ate it while I ran back to school. In college, it was the same thing—school one place, work another. I was always rushing, eating a piece of food on the run.

So most of my childhood was pretty much like that of millions of other working-class children of immigrants at the time. My days were filled with work and sports and hanging around with my

friends. My interests were centered on my family and my neighborhood. I had no great intellectual pursuits or dreams for the future
other than that maybe someday I might be a basketball star.

But two things brought me out of this cocoon. The first was my
brothers' band. And the second was politics.

WHEN I was in junior high school, Phil and Jack and their friends
had started a band. Phil played saxophone and Jack was on drums.
It wasn't just for fun, like kids do now. They saw it as a way to make
money. Before long they were going up to the Catskills in the summer, playing at small hotels like the Royalton House in Monticello.
In those days all of Jewish New York dreamed of spending summers
in "the mountains," which to them meant the hotels and cottages in
the southern Catskill region along what is now Route 17.

When my brothers' band got summer work up there, my parents
would rent a bungalow in Mountaindale or some other nearby
place. Once in a while they would let me go to the hotel to hear the
band. At that time you didn't just play in the band, you had to provide entertainment too. I would watch and admire them. They had a
witty piano player who was very funny. That was the greatest
thing—to be able to be in a band and do the show and have fun
with skits and sketches and punch lines. The larger hotels like the
Flagler or the Nevele had social staffs and entertainment in addition
to the bands. The comedians Smith and Dale, with their "Dr.
Cronkite" and restaurant routines, were a favorite. I was very interested in that kind of thing.

When I got back to the city I'd go to the Palace Theater in Times
Square on Saturday afternoons. They had all the big acts—Burns
and Allen, Jack Benny, the Marx Brothers, the young Milton Berle,
and an even younger Bob Hope. I would go and take notes on what
they said, and then I would send letters to my brothers in the
Catskills with gags they could use in their sketches. Sometimes I
would memorize acts. I knew all the jokes. When Sammy Levenson
became friendly with us, I used to keep a notebook with punch
lines. I once had more than four hundred of them. Most were
Sammy's.

After a while, Phil and Jack said I should learn an instrument so I could join the band and make money for college. They suggested tenor saxophone since Phil played alto. I began taking lessons, and when I went to the Palace I started paying more attention to the bands. I followed them all, particularly Paul Whiteman's big band. Whiteman hired the best white jazz musicians, like Bix Beiderbecke on trumpet, Frankie Trumbauer on sax, Jack Teagarden on trombone, and Ferde Grofe at the piano. He also had Bing Crosby and the Rhythm Boys. It was like going to a concert. Whiteman introduced classics like George Gershwin's "Rhapsody in Blue." I'd follow them wherever they played. I'd catch them at the Palace, the Brooklyn Paramount, or the Fox or Strand.

I wasn't really good on the saxophone, but then to be a band at a small hotel in the Catskills, you didn't have to be good. Many bands weren't, including ours. As a matter of fact, people who listened to us and knew of Phil and Jack's reputations as scholars said we played wisely but not well.

At first I'd occasionally sit in with my brothers' band at dances in the city. I wouldn't get paid, but I got some experience. Sometimes I'd get jobs on my own for New Year's Eve. You'd go that morning to the Sam Asch music store on Pitkin Avenue in Brooklyn where the bandleaders hung out. You'd wear a symbol to identify yourself. Since I played sax, I'd stick a reed in my hatband or lapel. The negotiations were tricky. When you asked a bandleader, "How much?" he might say, "Five dollars" but raise two fingers. That meant he got five dollars per band member but paid only two dollars.

Then toward the end of high school, my brothers started including me up in the mountains. Henry would be there too, playing alto sax. Phil and Jack would let me be master of ceremonies once in a while. Then one summer I was offered the job of social director at the Arrowhead Lodge in Ellenville. I found that I had absorbed all I'd been watching and listening to through the years, and I could do my version of it on stage as emcee. The season was a big success, and I knew I'd found a niche for myself.

It was at one of our shows at Arrowhead that Sammy Levenson first performed for money. We knew he was funny, and we convinced him to try it on stage. He was a big hit and got a job there the next summer.

The band became a big part of my life. You made money, you had fun, you met girls. That was my social life. A great thing to do.

Henry and I became devoted tennis players in the Catskills and came to regard decent courts as a requirement for taking a job for the band. We were dismayed, therefore, to find after we'd agreed to a summer at the Saxon Hotel near Monticello that management had grossly exaggerated its facilities. No playable tennis courts. Our dilemma was that the contract we'd signed, written on a paper bag in which I'd brought my lunch for the audition, provided that we could be fired but couldn't quit. We devised a plan with the rest of the band. One Saturday night, each of us took out music for a different number. The boss walked in with a favorite perennial guest on his arm while we were separately playing a waltz, a rumba, a fox trot, and a tango. We hoped he'd fire us. But he listened for a moment, then turned to the guest and said, "You see, when they want to they can play!" We finished the season at the Saxon.

Later we became a more political band. Our theme song was "Joe Hill." One of our highlights was when we got a job playing for the Republican Party at the Cornish Arms Hotel in New York City. When ultraconservative Congressman Hamilton Fish (President Franklin Roosevelt's Hyde Park neighbor and archenemy) walked in, we played "Red Sails in the Sunset." No one complained.

We warmed up for Louis Prima and Keely Smith once at an Office and Professional Employees International Union dance at Manhattan Center. They were a top band, and they all wore stylish crimson blazers. We used to insist, "We have uniforms too. We all wear maroon ties." I don't think Prima knew what to make of us, but that date went over okay.

Besides being fun, the band prepared me for a lot of things I did later in life. I became the person who lined up the jobs and found people who would perform with us. There were four of us Foners in the band and usually several other friends, so we had a lot of contacts. We knew a lot of people: people from the neighborhood, people from high school and college, people from politics. That gave us an advantage over other bands because we'd use those contacts to get us jobs. We'd also use them to find attractions to appear with our act, people just starting out like the singers Josh White or Leadbelly or comics Sammy or Irwin Corey ("The World's Foremost Authority") or Zero Mostel. Mostel, who later starred in the movie version of *The Producers*, made his first public appearance at one of our jobs—a dance run by the Newspaper Guild. I was comfortable talking to a lot of people, and I was energetic and persistent, so I got to do most of the job hunting and talent seeking, and the experience was very useful later when I worked for unions.

MY other new focus as I grew through my late teens was politics.

I had floated through high school and, because it seemed expected of me, enrolled in Brooklyn College in 1932. I played on the basketball team for the first two years, but I was losing interest. I wasn't that good, and maybe because Phil and Jack were basically out of the house, I didn't feel I had to hide away in sports anymore. For whatever reason, I was ready for something new.

I've already mentioned how apolitical my childhood was. Williamsburg wasn't the Lower East Side. It wasn't as poor, and people like us were more interested in moving up the ladder than changing the world. Throughout high school and my first couple of years in college I'd read the papers occasionally, but my interest in politics centered on the municipal scandals of the time. I remember following the Seabury Commission investigation of corruption in the regime of Mayor Jimmy Walker. Politics to me as a boy meant electing a Democrat, probably a corrupt one. You never heard of a Republican. There were leftists in our building, anarchists named Cooper who tried to interest our family in the Sacco and Vanzetti case. I remember vaguely that people said good things about the socialists like New York Congressman Meyer London, that they were for the people, the poor people. These things made no great impression on me at the time. But still, radicalism was in the air, and I must have absorbed some of it without thinking. My brother Jack remembered being taken as a boy to a rally to hear Eugene V. Debs speak. When I was a freshman in college, still primarily interested in basketball, I wrote an essay titled, "Don't Throw Away Your Vote: Vote for Norman Thomas." He was the Socialist Party candidate, so the idea must have come from somewhere.

My brothers were now in graduate school at Columbia, but they still knew people in the City College Registrar's office. They got me a job there. After my classes in downtown Brooklyn (that was where Brooklyn College was then), I'd get on the train to go to work at Convent Avenue and 138th Street in Manhattan. Sometimes, if there were a gap in time, I'd take a nap in a room the twins rented near the college.

This was New York City at the height of the Depression, and idealistic young people took sides passionately on issues such as unemployment, the growth of the CIO (Congress of Industrial Organizations), the rise of fascism, lynchings in the South, and so on. Phil and Jack were in the midst of this ferment and moving toward the Left. They took me aside one night and suggested I look beyond basketball, take an interest in the world, maybe read some articles in *The Nation* or the *New Republic* magazines.

By the time I started my junior year, it was 1934 and everyone I knew was getting concerned about the rise of Hitler in Germany. A lot of my friends were becoming active politically, joining the Young Communist League (YCL) and the American League Against War and Fascism. It seemed to me that the smartest and the best people were doing this, and while my background was apolitical, there also was nothing in it to make the Left seem horrible or un-American. I was meeting Communists in college and they were doing things like trying to unionize the faculty or campaigning to get a black history course taught by a black professor, and they were nice, law-abiding, principled people, and I said, "Why not?"

So somewhere around 1935 I joined the YCL and became active in all sorts of political issues. I'd be through with my Brooklyn College classes by early afternoon, take the train to Manhattan to my job at City College, and then go home to an evening of political phone calls. I remember spending a weekend with my brother Henry and Frank Herbst going from car to car on what's now the "N" train to Coney Island making speeches to try to get donations to help the Loyalists in the Spanish Civil War. Or we'd write songs and do skits and sketches to try to dramatize the issues and get people to join the YCL.

Sammy Levenson was not a political person but he watched us.

He made up a multiple-choice quiz on "What Is a Communist?" One of the correct answers was "Someone who has ten copies of the same pamphlet." Another was "Someone who wears lisle stockings." That was because after the Japanese invasion of Manchuria we were supposed to boycott silk. We wrote a song that went, "You'll be in style. Wear hose made of lisle." Henry almost got in trouble for writing a verse that went "It's a treat to be kissed by a young Communist."

We were young and optimistic. We were sure the world was moving toward a more just society, a socialist society. I didn't know much about unions until my brother Phil began getting invited to various union organizing conferences to lecture about U.S. labor history. He'd come back and tell us about it, and we'd get excited. It seemed that things were happening all around the country that were going to end economic injustice and make people's lives better. Even though our family didn't feel the effects of the Depression firsthand, we were certainly aware of the hunger marches, tenant battles, and farm foreclosures. We followed the San Francisco general strike in 1934 and the founding of the CIO and passage of the Wagner Act in 1935. We applauded the rapid organizing of auto, steel, and other basic industries in the late 1930s. We felt we were part of a worldwide movement for social change, and we were willing to work hard to help make that change happen.

I found I was good at political work. People liked me. They saw I was committed and willing to do as much or more work than anybody else. I think they thought I was smart, and that was because by this time I was doing a lot of reading. At Brooklyn College, my marks were going up because for the first time I was taking an interest and doing the assignments. I spent a lot of time on the train traveling to school and work, and I read the *Times,* the *Herald Tribune* and the *Daily Worker* every day and could remember and quote things in discussions. That impressed people. Also, I had a sense of humor, and that never hurts.

Of course, we on the Left made a lot of horrible mistakes and believed a lot of lies in those years—especially about the Soviet Union. Even at the beginning I'd read something in *The Nation* or the *New*

Republic that planted some doubt in my mind about a Communist Party position. But we were involved in so many good things that I'd put that doubt on hold and keep working to support strikers or fight racism or try to help stop Hitler. It wasn't until the Khrushchev revelations in 1956 about what went on under Stalin that I finally left the Party. But for many years before that, my doubts had been growing and I'd been moving further and further away from any real participation.

When I graduated Brooklyn College in 1936, I went from part time at the CCNY registrar's office to full time. I worked there until 1940, when an upstate New York legislator, George Rapp, and a conservative lawyer, Frederick Coudert, decided to campaign against what they saw as Communist subversion in New York City higher education. The mood of the country toward the Left had shifted after the Communists supported the Nazi–Soviet peace pact of 1939. We weren't as widely accepted, and the conservatives saw an opening. The Rapp–Coudert investigation was like a local warm-up for the House Un-American Activities Committee–type investigations of the postwar McCarthy era.

When the Rapp–Coudert hearings began in 1940, Phil and Jack were teaching American history at CCNY, I was working at CCNY, and Henry was a student there. We had been friendly with an evening session CCNY history instructor named William Canning. As a matter of fact, when he was out of work with no place to live, my parents took him in and fed him until he got back on his feet. Canning became an informer. He named us all as agents of a "plot" to use the schools for revolutionary propaganda. He was the main witness against us. My father was very angry. He remembered that he had gone to an optometrist to pick up (and pay for) Canning's glasses.

Phil, Jack, and I were suspended and then, in 1941, fired. In the unsuccessful protest campaign that followed, a group was formed called Friends of the Foners. It held a fund-raiser that my mother attended. She was very proud when she heard the song written for the occasion by Norman Franklin, a friend who was in the band with us. The chorus went:

Mrs. Foner had four sons—
Making a dent in the old exchequer—
Two single units and a double-decker.
Mrs. Foner had four sons,
And we're mighty proud of them all.

After we were suspended, we changed the name of our band to Suspended Swing. I achieved my first public relations coup when I got the *New York Post* columnist Leonard Lyons to include an item on the new name in his "Lyons Den" column.

A vindicating footnote to the Rapp–Coudert witch-hunt came in 1980 when the trustees of City University of New York (CUNY), the successor to the Board of Higher Education that had approved the firings, unanimously passed a resolution apologizing to the committee's victims, including some fifty of the city's finest teachers, who had been fired. The resolution pledged never to let such a violation of academic freedom happen again. The apology was nice, but it couldn't restore the ruined careers of so many able and dedicated scholars. Nor could it repair the damage done to freedom of inquiry.

Back in 1941, our preoccupation with the committee faded quickly. The reason was simple. By the end of the year, America was at war.

2. Sing While You Fight

Finding the Labor Movement

I GOT DRAFTED in 1943. Someone must have seen that I had been involved in entertainment and had been an emcee, because right after basic training at Fort Dix I was sent to Special Services at 65 Broadway in Manhattan and assigned to a company that was preparing the Irving Berlin show "This Is the Army" for the troops. It was directed by Kurt Kasnar and featured a lot of big names.

I was only there about a week when my records must have caught up with me. Kasnar came to me and said, "There's a problem. Because of your background you can't stay here. We'll send you to Governor's Island. If you want, we'll send you to the band there at Fort Jay."

"Don't send me to the band," I said.

I didn't want to spend the war playing music. So they sent me to the Governor's Island commissary instead. That was how I fought the war—as an inventory clerk who took the ferry from the middle of New York harbor and spent three nights a week in my wife's apartment on East 11th Street in Manhattan. (More about that in a minute.)

The commissary was for officers' food, and at the end of the month they'd want to keep the inventory down. "Get that stuff out of here," they'd tell us. This is at a time of shortages in everything, and I'm going home with the best steaks in the world. I gave one to my mother but she didn't know much about fancy steaks. She stewed it and made it like rubber.

But I did get injured during the war, sort of. I was on the post basketball team, and after one game I got a fantastic pain in my neck and down my arm. I went to the sick hall and spent the next nine months in hospitals being misdiagnosed. The other patients called me "Crooked Neck." Finally, a neurosurgeon at Halloran General Hospital on Staten Island said the problem was a cervical disk. They recommended surgery, an unusual procedure at the time. As they wheeled me into the operating room, someone asked if I wanted to see a rabbi.

"Does he know anything about neurosurgery?" I asked.

The operation was a success. Disk problems were cropping up a lot then. Many involved paratroopers. The doctors didn't know enough about the subject, so my case interested them. For weeks afterward, visiting surgeons would come to me and say, "Okay Corporal Foner, tell 'em how it used to be." And I'd go through my whole routine.

I was discharged from the Army in 1945.

Let me go back for a minute and tell about an important personal event. I had drifted for a couple of years after I was fired from my job at City College. I had my political work, and I made some money with the band. But I was in my mid-twenties and essentially unemployed and living at home, which by then was with my parents in Boro Park.

However, one good thing happened to me in that period. I courted a lovely young woman named Anne Berman, and we got married. I'd known Anne slightly from the American Student Union (ASU), a national group involved in many left and liberal causes. Anne, who was an economics major at Queens College, was active in it. But we were only acquaintances.

The band had a job in the summer of 1939 at Blue Mountain Lodge in Peekskill, New York. One night I looked across the dance floor and saw Anne, who was visiting with a friend. She was attractive and vivacious. I asked the rest of the band if they could play without me for a while, and I went over and asked her to dance. It was a fox-trot, and that's when our courtship began.

For the next two years I pursued her in the city. I'd borrow my father's car in Boro Park and drive over to visit her at her parents' home in Flushing, which was now residential and no longer farm country. I had no job, but her family seemed to have confidence in me.

In December of 1941, around the time of Pearl Harbor, we got married. Anne has never forgotten our "honeymoon." She may have forgiven, but she hasn't forgotten. It was Christmas and the band had a week-long engagement for a Teachers Union event at Arrowhead Lodge. The lodge was filled, so they put us up nearby at Kleinmans, a rooming house owned by relatives of Harold Leventhal, the music promoter. But Kleinmans was crowded too. It was like open house in a dormitory, with people running in and out. I was away all the time playing at Arrowhead, and the teachers were occupied with themselves and ignored Anne. And that was our honeymoon.

It may sound like a funny story, but it's not really so funny. The honeymoon was a little like the next sixty years. We were both committed people, anything for the cause. But the way it worked out was that I was away at work too much of the time and Anne had the major responsibility for the home and the two daughters that came along. Anne is a very, very capable person, and eventually she got a Ph.D. in sociology and had a successful scholarly career at Rutgers. But the arrangement we had for many years was not fair to her and it also deprived our daughters of time with their father at important periods when they were growing up. I was committed to trying to be a good husband and father, but at some important stages I wasn't always present. That's one of the big regrets I have as I look back on my life.

After I got out of the Army in 1945, we lived for a while with Anne's parents in Flushing. Later that year our daughter Nancy was born and we got our own apartment in Queens. For a couple of years I had a job packing and shipping woolens while I played in the band and did political work on the side.

On Lincoln's Birthday weekend in 1947 we were playing at Arrowhead Lodge again. One of the guests was Nick Carnes, president of Local 1250, one of several department store unions in New York at that time. I had done some education courses for Local 1250 members, so he knew me.

Nick played the guitar and was studying sax. In the intermission he came up and said, "How would you like to be education director for 1250? If you take the job we can play duets."

That's how I joined the labor movement.

My work at first was giving labor history and union education classes, putting out a bulletin, doing leaflets, that sort of thing. We represented workers at Hearn's, Namm's, Loeser's, Oppenheim-Collins, Norton's—all stores that have since disappeared. I used to say we had the Midas touch in reverse. I was looking for a chance to do something new when I found out that Local 1250 and Local 5, which paid part of my salary, were in a loose department store council with other locals that represented workers at Macy's, Gimbels, and other big stores. These locals all together had about eighteen thousand members. That was large enough for an idea I'd been toying with.

I proposed that we do an original musical revue. The locals agreed, and each put in a small amount of money. I got my brother Henry and Norman Franklin from the band to agree to write the songs and sketches. Then I went to Liz Lampell, a Local 1250 organizer whose husband Millard Lampell was on his way to becoming a well-known Hollywood screenwriter. Millard helped me set up an advisory board. On it were Millard and others who were also on their way to becoming well known, including the playwright Arthur Miller and film producer/director Martin Ritt, who later directed *Norma Rae* and other Academy Award-winning movies.

Through the band and our political work I had access to an unusually large number of creative people who were, because of their political beliefs, more than happy to participate for little or no money in union cultural events. It was part of the times. These were people who, like my brothers and myself, were caught up in the hope that we could build a better world. Culture was to some extent a weapon in that effort. The Left had created a vigorous cultural life that became part of its mass appeal. The most famous writers of the 1930s—Ernest Hemingway, John Dos Passos, Thomas Wolfe, Federico Garcia Lorca, William Saroyan, Langston Hughes, Richard Wright, S. J. Perelman, James Agee, Theodore Dreiser, Malcolm Cowley—appeared in the *New Masses* magazine, which was close to the Communist Party. The *Daily Worker* had great cartoons by people like Robert Minor, William Gropper, and Art Young, but artists from the *New Yorker* also appeared there. This was the era of the experimental Group Theater and what we used to call "socially significant" plays like *Waiting for Lefty*, the Clifford Odets play about striking taxi drivers, which moved me deeply when I saw it in 1935. The International Ladies Garment Workers Union had already put on its immensely successful musical revue "Pins and Needles," and on a smaller scale, the American Student Union put on a musical every year. One of them, called "Pens and Pencils," was a takeoff on the Marx Brothers. I raised one hundred dollars to finance it when I was working at City College. There was a Theater Arts Committee that had a cabaret to support the Loyalists in the Spanish Civil War. And the YCL was always putting on skits and shows.

I had lived and worked in the middle of this tradition for more than a dozen years, and I was already friendly with theater people like Lampell, Miller, Ritt, Sam Levenson, Zero Mostel, comic Irwin Corey, the actors John Randolph and Jack Gilford, the playwright Norman Rosten, the future television writer Mel Tolkin, the monologist Les Pine and many others. So it wasn't unusual that I would think of putting on a musical revue for the department store unions. Nor was it unusual that I would think I could get help from some of my friends.

We named the show *Thursdays 'Til Nine*, based on the fact that department stores stayed open until nine o'clock only on Thursdays. The plot was built around a store worker who can't find a place to live because of the postwar housing shortage and ends up living in the store at night. The store's owner—R. H. Maybe ("Don't Say No—Say Maybe!") announces a prize of a new home for the employee who writes the best musical number about the store. The hero, knowing on which side his bread is buttered, writes a song in which the store is an idyllic enterprise that the workers can't wait to get to on Monday mornings. Scorned by his fellow employees for "selling out" and in danger of losing his girl, he sees the error of his ways. His song wins the contest, but at the presentation ceremony he sings, instead, a song called "Selling Union" which makes the case that "without the help of a worker's hand, the store is without a heart," and "without the help of the union's hand, you're finished before you start." The show's seventeen songs included "The Ballad of the Bra," "It's Closing Time," "How Long the Day," "Fifteen Minute Relief" and "The Taft–Hartley Rumba," the latter a shot at the recently passed antilabor Taft–Hartley Act.

We knew our stuff had to be good and it had to be topical, but it couldn't be too narrow. If we focused on the union's immediate contract fights, we ran the risk of becoming dated and boring. We had to aim at broader, more ongoing themes.

Many department store workers of that era were aspiring actors. When we put out a call for auditions, four hundred members showed up. A couple were ringers—experienced actors for whom we got jobs in the industry. But the rest were real. We chose fifty for the cast and rehearsed four times a week for six weeks. Here they were, young people spending all that time together on a union project and having a good time doing it. It was a great experience, like going to summer camp. And you can imagine what it did for their identification with the union.

We booked the show for a Sunday preview and four nights at the Central Needle Trades High School on West 24th Street in Manhattan. We invited all the critics and important people from Broadway to the preview: Irving Berlin, Harold Rome, you name it, they were there. I sat in the balcony with Bill Michelson, the head of Local 2, one of the sponsoring locals. When the curtain came down there was a standing ovation. All those big shots gave it ten curtain calls!

"My God, I can't believe it's that good," I said.

"I guess we'll have to take it to Broadway," said Michelson.

Michelson was serious, but nothing like that happened. "Thursdays" closed after five performances. But it was a sensation among the members. Six thousand—or one out of three of them—saw it. It was reviewed in the *New York Times* and other daily and labor papers. I was interviewed about it on *Luncheon at Sardi's*, which was then a popular radio show about show business. A couple of months later I got a call from Dumont TV, then New York's only television station. They wanted to film the show. But there was no way. We had thrown out all the sets, costumes, and other stuff because we had no storage space. The cast was dispersed and back at work.

"The only way you can film it is if you've got a shovel," I told Dumont.

Because most of the outside talent was donated, "Thursdays" cost at most a couple of thousand dollars. It would have cost less if we had been able to apply ticket receipts against expenses, but in order to get the use of the high school theater, we had to donate the proceeds to a worthy cause—in this case the Disabled Veterans of America. For that couple of thousand dollars, though, the union reaped immense rewards in good publicity, education on labor issues, and membership pride in their union.

For me personally, "Thursdays" provided many important lessons that I used later in producing the even more successful musical revue *Take Care* for Local 1199.

Unfortunately, Local 1250 wasn't able to follow through on "Thursdays" and build a vigorous cultural program. One reason was that 1250 wasn't big enough. You need a union with a lot of members to provide participants and audiences for major cultural programming. But the most important reason was that 1250 was independent and was being raided by other unions. We spent most of the time defending ourselves. For me, that meant putting out a lot of literature.

By this time our headquarters were at 13 Astor Place in lower Manhattan. Lots of other unions were in that building too, including Local 144, which was a graphic display union. That's where I first met Stanley Glaubach, an artist who was a member of 144. He was a brilliant, wonderful man who became tops in his field, creating covers for *Time* magazine and designing many labor publications before his tragic death of a heart attack in 1973 at the age of 49.

Stan introduced me to the concept of good graphics. Although I couldn't type, and can't to this day, I had learned to write passable copy for leaflets and brochures in longhand. But I had no idea how to design things. When you're trying to educate people and motivate them into action, you could write the Gettysburg Address and if it looks uninviting and all gray on the page, most of the people who get the leaflet won't read it. Stan made this point to me, and I've never forgotten it.

We worked together on a booklet. I forget the subject, but it was a beautifully designed thing. It was two colors, and inside on each page was a good sharp picture of a member with a statement in big type and bigger quotation marks. Lots of white space. It made a big impact. With Stanley's influence pushing me forward, I found a cartoonist in from the West Coast and had him do a cartoon history of our union. Of course, Ben Shahn had done a lot of posters for the CIO, so we had a general idea that visual art had a role in union life, but meeting Stan Glaubach helped make that concept real for me.

Working with Stan also underlined another important concept. My theory in working with artists and creative people of any kind is to try to get the very best and then trust them and stay out of their way. By the very best, I mean talented people who also have a feel for your basic goals, who in some way share your worldview. Once you have those people and have made clear what you want, leave them alone. There is no such thing as genius by committee. Talented people will not do good work if officials are constantly looking over their shoulders, and you're not likely to get their services a second time. But if you establish a reputation as someone who they can work with, and if they are among the many creative people who have a feel for the underdog, you may find them ready to donate their talents for your projects over and over again. I learned not to be shy about asking.

I mentioned that we'd moved to 13 Astor Place. The reason was that in February 1950, department store Locals 1250 and 5 were absorbed by District 65, which owned the whole ten-story building on Astor Place.

District 65 at that time represented about twenty thousand workers in what they called the distributive, or wholesale and warehouse, industry. It was the center of left unionism in New York. Its headquarters on Astor Place was a beehive of activity. They had classes of every description. They had a consumer service, which, because of the industry they were in, offered goods cheaply. They had rallies, dances, dramatic groups, choruses, entertainment, children's programs, and a cafeteria. Meetings were going on all the time. Every night the building was hopping. Most of the members at that time lived in Manhattan. It was easy for them to go from work to the union hall. For a lot of members, 65 was the center of their lives. That was especially true of members who bought into the union's broad social justice commitment. You'd come there and hear slogans like "Life with a Purpose" and "Sing While You Fight," and you'd really get inspired.

When we became part of 65 I was put in charge of all of its education, social, and cultural programs. One of the things I did was start a nightclub on the building's top floor. It was open every Saturday night except for the summer—we had no air-conditioning. Each week a different group of members would be in charge of selling 400 tickets at fifty cents each. Rank-and-file committees would set up, check coats, wait on tables, serve drinks, etc. The dramatic group would be responsible for a variety show. I'd line up a band. And every Saturday night I'd get a guest star to perform for free. Among them were Sammy Levenson, Jack Gilford, Zero Mostel, and Irwin Corey. Harry Belafonte was just breaking in then, and he'd come down and sing in his dark glasses. We were packing them in, the place was always full. We called it the "65 Saturday Nite Club."

Also on Saturdays, we had the kiddy program. I'd get magicians and puppeteers. Pete Seeger and Woody Guthrie would sing. Sometimes Guthrie brought his wife Margie to do dance programs. One Saturday, one of the magicians, Doc Horowitz, took me aside.

"Moe," he said, "You're doing too much. You plan everything, you set up the chairs, you're the master of ceremonies, afterwards you clean up. You should get my daughter to be the emcee."

Doc's daughter was twelve years old, but she was already a terrific ventriloquist and puppeteer with stage skills far in advance of her years. She made a wonderful emcee for us. Later she became a fixture in children's TV programs as Shari Lewis.

We also ran boat rides. We'd sell out two boats and go up the Hudson to Bear Mountain or Indian Point and spend the entire day with all kinds of organized programs. We had ball games and shows—everything for everybody.

The 1949 Paul Robeson concert at Peekskill happened while I was at 65, and we played a role in it. The great African American actor and bass singer was being demonized in the press for his leftist politics when his outdoor concert was announced that August. Vigilantes mobilized by right-wing groups broke up the originally scheduled concert even before it could begin. The concert was rescheduled for a week later, and four thousand men from left unions—many of them 65ers—formed a human circle around the event to protect Robeson and the big audience. The concert went off without incident, but leaving the grounds up a long narrow dirt road was a nightmare. We sort of knew the vigilantes were waiting, but we still had to get out. As we drove, people who were lined up all along the road yelled at us and threw rocks. The police stood by but did nothing to protect us. I think one rioter was arrested. I had filled my car with people, most from 65, and told them, "You just lie flat and I'll keep driving." Every window in my car was smashed, and glass flew everywhere. Many concertgoers were seriously hurt, but none in my car. It took me days to get the glass out of my hair. For years and years afterward the people that were in my car exchanged Christmas cards.

So I was going crazy with all the activity at 65, but it was such excitement. Every Saturday morning at nine there would be a staff meeting. Arthur Osman was the founder and president of 65 and David Livingston was the number two man. Later, Cleve Robinson was president, but not while I was there. Osman was an organizational genius, and Livingston was brilliant too. If you just sat there and breathed at those staff meetings, you'd absorb stuff.

Osman was also a little crazy and a regular tyrant. As soon as I got there, he had me rewrite a report ten times. Change this, change that. It was like he was playing with me, making me jump through hoops to show who was in charge. But I learned a lot about how to run a union and involve workers from him and Livingston. District 65 was centralized but democratic. The leadership came from the ranks. There was a shop steward structure, with steward meetings every month. A lot of people were involved in making decisions and carrying them out.

At 65, you learned about finances. You couldn't just piss money away, things had to pay for themselves. That's how I became frugal. At 65, the organizers worked their asses off. They were proud of their union, and they admired and respected their leaders. They also feared them. Both Osman and Livingston criticized people right and left, and they were brutal if you tried to argue. They'd destroy you in public. Still, I think 65's pluses outweighed its minuses. It was an eye-opener for me. Much, if not most, of what I know about labor I learned at 65.

So at 65 I'd work until ten or eleven at night every weekday, and I still couldn't wait to get to those 9 A.M. Saturday staff meetings. I hated to leave at eleven when I had to prepare for the children's programs. After they were over, I'd start with the Saturday Nite Club, and I wouldn't get home until three or four in the morning. I'd sleep all day Sunday and start all over again Monday morning. We felt like we were saving the world, but my family lost out.

While all this was going on there was tremendous turmoil in the left sector of the labor movement, which was then quite large. The turmoil centered around the Taft–Hartley Act of 1947. There had been a surge of organizing and strikes after the war. A left-led union, the United Electrical Workers under Jim Matles and Julius Emspak, came out of nowhere and had half a million members. Harry Bridges' longshore union was growing on the West Coast. Other left-led unions included the Mine, Mill, and Smelter Workers, the Transport Workers, the Food and Agricultural Workers, the Furriers, and many others.

As the Cold War escalated, pressure in Congress to curb labor resulted in the Taft-Hartley Act. Among its provisions was a requirement that officers of labor unions sign non-Communist affidavits. This split the Left into two camps. One camp said if you're a Communist, resign from the Party and sign. Otherwise your union will be kicked out of the AFL (American Federation of Labor) or CIO (Congress of Industrial Organizations)—these federations didn't merge until 1955—and you'll be raided and destroyed. The other camp said refuse to sign. You'll get kicked out and you'll get raided, but if you fight hard you'll survive with your integrity intact.

The Communist Party was in the latter camp. The leaders of District 65 were in the former. Pressure to implement the Taft–Hartley affidavits began in 1948, and the internal debate at 65 was white-hot. Some close friendships were destroyed for life. The Communists were strong within the union, but Osman and Livingston were, of course, in power. Most union leaders, even if they sympathize with an outside organization, don't like being told by outsiders what to do. In this case, Osman and Livingston did what they thought best for 65. They signed the non-Communist affidavits and stayed in the CIO.

I was caught in the middle of this debate, an excruciating position. I agreed with Osman and Livingston. I wanted 65 to survive inside the House of Labor and live to fight another day. But most of my family disagreed. They saw Taft–Hartley as a dangerous infringement of civil liberties that no person of conscience could submit to. I was torn, and Osman and Livingston saw that. Gradually, they took away my responsibilities. They were signaling me that I could stay for a while, but I'd have to leave eventually.

Local 1199 at this time was a five thousand–member pharmacy union that resembled 65 in many respects. In an informal way it was in 65's orbit. Leon Davis, 1199's founder and president, sometimes came to 65 staff meetings just to hear what was going on. It happened that both Davis and I lived in the Bayside section of Queens and took our daughters to the same storefront Jewish Sunday school. It was the kind of place where Jewish kids learned about Harriet Tubman and Sojourner Truth. My daughter Nancy still remembers learning there that Tubman was the Moses of her people.

Davis had decided like Osman and Livingston to sign the non-Communist affidavit. But the battle was nowhere near so fierce in 1199 as in 65. The members basically went along with Davis's decision. Everything I knew about 1199 was positive—it was small but honest, principled, efficient, and militant. And it was not at this point torn by internal dissension.

While our daughters were in class, Davis would say, "Why don't we walk around?" He'd usually ask me what was happening in 65.

One Sunday I told him about the Taft–Hartley debate.

"I think Osman and Livingston are right, but I'm going to leave," I said.

"Where will you go?" he asked.

"I don't know. Someone told me I should learn typesetting and get a job as a printer."

Davis was silent for a minute. Then he said, "How would you like to come work for us? You could put out our magazine, things like that."

Thinking how small 1199 was, I said, "How could you pay me? I make sixty-five dollars a week."

"Don't worry," said Davis. "It's a deal." I started work at 1199 in September 1952. When I got there, I found everybody else was getting ninety dollars a week. But I've never regretted the move.

3. Grab Them by the Collar

Telling the Story
of Forgotten Workers

LOCAL 1199 was twenty years old when I came on staff in 1952. It was formed in 1932 by the merger of the Pharmacists Union of Greater New York (one visitor described this organization's headquarters as "a sloppy cubbyhole with four guys playing chess") and the New York Drug Clerks Association (described by Leon Davis as "highly sectarian and with no substantial following").

The new union was called Local 1199, Retail Drug Employees Union. Davis, a drug clerk who had immigrated at the age of fifteen from what is now Belarus (White Russia), was one of its founders. Dave, which is what we always called him, was a remarkable man. He had very little formal education, but I think history will remember him as one of the twentieth century's most important leaders of working people. I think of him among labor leaders such as CIO founder John L. Lewis, Walter Reuther in his early days with the Auto Workers, former New York City Central Labor Council President Harry Van Arsdale, Harry Bridges of the West Coast longshoremen, and Jim Matles and Julius Emspak of the United Electrical Workers.

Davis was selfless. He was never interested in getting more money for himself. His concern was the members of the union, all the time. If members went to jail or didn't get paid during a strike, Dave went to jail and gave up his salary, and made the staff do the same. One of the signs of his greatness was his close identification with working people. Our rule was that no union officer or staff member could make more than the highest-paid union member. As a matter of fact, in later years Davis made substantially less than many members who were skilled hospital professionals. The staff got the same raises that were negotiated for the members. The only time I can remember Davis taking an anti-union stance was when staff members talked of unionizing. It didn't happen. As a result, as we grew our salary scale was low for unions of our size. No one ever got rich working at 1199. The idea was that you worked there out of principle.

Davis was also a master strategist. He'd sit in his office, sometimes for hours, just staring straight ahead. You'd think, "Maybe he's napping." But no, he was imagining three years into the future, what was going to happen and what he should do about it. That's how he came up with ideas like the prepaid prescription drug plan, building our Benefit and Pension Funds, creating our Training Fund, and organizing hospital workers nationally.

He could be merciless with the staff. He'd yell at people and the standard reaction was just, "That's the way he is. He screams at everyone." But he didn't yell at me. I was fortunate that he was receptive to my ideas and usually let me alone to carry them out. Also, Dave stayed away from the limelight. He was self-conscious about his Russian accent and didn't like to talk with reporters or celebrities. He was glad to let me do that.

PARTLY because of Davis and partly because the early 1199 was built mostly by people with left political backgrounds similar to his, the union I joined in 1952 was built on solid principles that proved to be important when the union moved from pharmacies to hospitals in the late 1950s. I'll mention a few:

The early 1199 stressed solidarity among all kinds of members. This was despite the fact that the union was overwhelmingly composed of Jewish men. 1199's inclusiveness was both a tactical recognition of the need for unity in fighting the boss and a part of the American Left's active opposition to racism and ethnic prejudice.

1199 successfully campaigned in Harlem in 1937 for hiring of black pharmacists. You had black pharmacists with degrees working back then as porters or in the post office. 1199 regularly denounced racial discrimination and was one of the earliest unions to celebrate Negro History Week. Some of the early black members were deeply committed to the union. So when 1199 began organizing primarily black and Hispanic hospital workers in the late 1950s, it already had a track record of civil rights commitment.

The early 1199 was part of the movement toward industrial unionism that resulted in the formation of the Congress of Industrial Organizations (CIO) in 1935. The earlier American Federation of Labor (AFL) was craft-oriented, which led to the initial existence in drugstores of separate unions for clerks and pharmacists. 1199 believed more could be accomplished if all the employees in an industry were organized into the same union. In a drugstore this meant getting the pharmacists, drug clerks, stockmen, soda men, and cosmeticians to think "all for one, and one for all." Not always easy, but 1199's experience in trying to build this kind of attitude became especially important when the union was faced with the highly diverse and stratified hospital industry.

The early 1199 was a militant union that relied on member participation. It was battle-tested after several bitter strikes at the Whelan drugstore chain. It had won contracts that raised wages and shortened hours. Part of the union's reliance on member participation in these efforts resulted from the industry's structure. New York had more than two thousand drugstores. This was before the dominance of big drugstore chains, and most stores were small, averaging one-and-a-half employees who often worked side by side with the boss. By the 1950s, 1199 had organized 80 percent of these stores. There was no way a small union staff could have organized and serviced all these stores by itself. Members had to participate, getting recruits worker by worker through conversations about local issues that might differ from neighborhood to neighborhood. When stores were organized, the role of elected rank-and-file local leaders (called delegates in 1199 and shop stewards in many other unions) was heightened by the isolated, decentralized nature of the industry. This reliance on member involvement later enabled the union to surprise onlookers by organizing large numbers of hospital workers in just a few years. Also, if you ask members to work hard for their union, you can't easily exclude them from decisions on union policy. So member participation was linked to internal democracy.

Finally, the early 1199 leadership was pretty sophisticated about not getting too far out in front of the members on political questions. The union had survived rough internal fights and official red-baiting, and Davis was dead-set against taking "feel-good" positions that didn't have much impact outside the union but might divide members. He was highly principled, but he understood the value of unity. He picked his battles. He made sure that before the union took a political position there was lots of open discussion and some kind of a consensus reached that was reflected in a vote by the members or their elected representatives.

MY duties when I started at 1199 in 1952 were to put out the publication and develop the social, cultural, and educational programs. The publication was a sixteen-page monthly magazine on glossy paper with a two-color cover. I didn't have the slightest idea of how to do it, and I was scared silly. But Marty Solow, a friend who was in advertising (he later had a major advertising agency) said, "I'll help you. You come out to my house on Long Island with the stories and I'll show you how we do it." I'd bring my handwritten stories, and he'd go over them. He'd improve the writing and show me how to do headlines. He'd tell me about getting the facts, news judgment, human interest angles, and such journalistic things.

Then Stanley Glaubach said, "Don't worry. I'll be the designer." I'd take the stories and photos over to Stan, and he'd sketch out layouts that made it look exciting, practically forcing you to turn the pages and read it. Also, my imagination, new ideas like adding more satire and cultural coverage, helped. After a while I was learning how to put out a publication, and the magazine was becoming much better than it had been. That's when *1199 News* started winning awards from the AFL-CIO's International Labor Communications Association and organizations like that. We've won hundreds of those prizes. I don't think any labor publication has been recognized for excellence as consistently as we have over the years.

After my first few years we hired additional staff for the magazine, and I became executive editor. I supervised the magazine but did less and less daily hands-on work. But I had formed my ideas on what makes a good labor paper, and I think they still hold up. I discuss them in chapter 8.

ONE of the first things I did at 1199 was to ask for help in developing cultural events from friends like Madeline Gilford, Jack Gilford's wife. I knew her from the student movement. She told me:

"There's a couple you've got to meet. He's working in the post office. His name is Ossie Davis. His wife is Ruby Dee, the actress."

Ossie and Ruby had worked in the play *The World of Sholom Aleichem* with friends of mine. I called them, we got together, and they agreed to help out. The first thing Ossie did for us was to write and direct a dramatic sketch about the cases that led to *Brown v. Board of Education*, the historic 1954 Supreme Court decision on school integration. A full house of 1199ers who paid fifty cents per head admission was deeply moved by the performance. The next year Ossie did a living newspaper dramatization for us on the lynching in Mississippi of Emmett Till, a black teenager. On another occasion I remember coming to the office and finding Ossie supervising a rehearsal of a cast that included Ruby, Harry Belafonte, Sidney Poitier, Will Geer, and Ricardo Montalban. One of the actors took me aside and said, "There's no one in the world who could get all these people together to do this—except Ossie."

That 1956 performance was also a big success and evolved into the annual 1199 Salute to Freedom. The auditoriums got bigger and bigger as we grew, but Ossie and Ruby were always at the center of the event as their connection with 1199 grew warmer and deeper. Salute to Freedom guests over the years included Dr. Martin Luther King, Jr., Coretta King, the Reverend Ralph Abernathy, Dick Gregory, Maya Angelou, Pete Seeger, Max Roach, Miriam Makeba, Mahalia Jackson, Stevie Wonder, and the casts of *The Wiz* and *Raisin*. Dr. King called 1199 "my favorite union" at the 1968 Salute, his last New York appearance.

My collaboration with Ossie and Ruby developed into close friendship, one I treasure. In their 1998 memoir *With Ossie and Ruby*, they refer to our relationship as "one of the most fruitful and rewarding associations of our lives." They add that 1199's "progressive policies on race and gender equality made it a pioneer. . . . In more ways than one Ruby and I, except for paying dues, consider ourselves members of 1199." Besides the Salute to Freedom, we developed events like the big Christmas kiddy program, a Salute to Israel, and a Latin American fiesta. We showed movies like *Salt of the Earth*, *The Organizer*, and Chaplin films. We had Teen Time events with square dances and guests like Eleanor Roosevelt, singer Sammy Davis, Jr., Slater Martin of the New York Knicks, and actors Sal Mineo, Lee Grant, and Tom Ewell. We held discussions with speakers such as Rep. Adam Clayton Powell, future Supreme Court Justice Thurgood Marshall, and socialist leaders Norman Thomas and Michael Harrington. My brother Phil spoke on labor history.

We ran all kinds of classes, from drugstore Spanish to how to sell cosmetics. We made a documentary film about drugstore workers. We started camp and scholarship programs for members' children. Thousands of 1199 kids and millions of dollars are now involved in these programs, but then it was a new idea that started small.

On one of our lecture nights, John Henry Faulk, a raconteur, was our speaker. His homespun Texas humor had been big on CBS radio, and he was starting to get into television when he was blacklisted. He sued and eventually won in the Supreme Court. He did this bit for us about being introduced to a Texas audience by his rabidly anti-Communist cousin Elmer.

"There's two things I want to say about John Henry," said cousin Elmer. "First, John Henry ain't ever been to the penitentiary, and second, I don't know why."

1199's decision to try to organize hospitals came in 1957. Until that point voluntary (private, nonprofit) hospitals around the country were largely unorganized. This was partly because they were excluded from collective bargaining coverage under the National Labor Relations Act of 1935. This law, known as the Wagner Act, gave almost all other workers in the country the right to organize and negotiate contracts within certain rules administered by the National Labor Relations Board (NLRB). The argument for exclusion of voluntary hospitals from the law was that many of these institutions were run by charitable organizations and church groups. Because their pay was so low, this put hospital workers in the position of being involuntary philanthropists.

The Wagner Act wasn't amended to include voluntary hospitals and nursing homes until July 11, 1974. By that time, however, ten states had extended union rights under state law to all hospital workers. As the result of 1199's efforts, New York became one of those ten states in 1965.

Another reason hospital workers were unorganized was that in major cities like New York, most were extremely low-paid minority women. Most unions weren't interested in organizing such workers. It meant devoting vast resources to a risky effort that would, even if successful, mean a low return in dues and a new kind of membership that most unions were unaccustomed—or even unwilling—to deal with.

Because hospital workers were ignored by the law and by the labor movement, we started calling them the "forgotten workers."

One day in late 1957, a short, near-sighted pharmacist showed up in the 1199 hiring hall looking for a job in a drugstore. His name was Elliott Godoff, and he was one of the most skilled union organizers of his day. Godoff, who came to this country from Russia in 1923 at the age of fifteen, had been trying to organize hospital workers since he went to work in 1935 at Israel Zion (now Maimonides) Hospital in Brooklyn. He'd been a full-time organizer since 1938 for the United Public Workers, the American Federation of State, County and Municipal Employees (AFSCME), and the Teamsters. For much of that time he worked with my boyhood friend Frank Herbst. For various reasons, including red-baiting, he'd had limited success. On that day in 1957, he'd just been let go by Teamsters Local 237 in New York and had decided to take a drugstore job for a while and regroup.

As Godoff sat there, Leon Davis walked by. The two knew each other, and Dave asked Godoff into his office for a chat. The result of that conversation was historic. Davis asked Godoff if he was willing to come to work for 1199 and take a crack at organizing hospitals.

When Godoff agreed, Dave took it to the other officers, the staff, and the delegate assemblies. It says a lot about the 1199 of that day that there was near-unanimous agreement to undertake a challenge that they all knew would require lots of effort and sacrifice. The drugstore members were pretty surprised a decade later to find they were dwarfed by the hospital membership. But most were terrifically proud at what their decision in 1957 had led to.

Godoff's first hospital campaign with 1199 was at Montefiore in the Bronx. He was assigned to go there with Teddy Mitchell, a North Carolina–born former drugstore porter who became 1199's first black vice president. Working with them, at first as a volunteer, was Marshall Dubin. Dubin was a lab technician who'd worked with Godoff before and later wrote a book of union poems that we put out under the title, *Talking with My Feet.*

Our target at Montefiore was the nine hundred service and maintenance workers, aides, orderlies, porters, clerks, and dietary workers who do the hard, unglamorous work in a hospital. Most were black and Puerto Rican women.

Godoff was a patient, gentle man who knew an enormous amount about organizing hospitals. He knew exactly what people did in the different jobs. He knew how to find the natural leaders in each department and get their help in organizing departmental committees. He knew how to listen and make suggestions without being overpowering. He knew how to inspire people and still not act like a know-it-all hotshot. He knew how to test workers to see what they were ready to do.

We established a headquarters near the hospital for meetings. Godoff and Mitchell practically lived there for a whole year. We handed out lots of leaflets. Stan Glaubach helped me with one particularly effective leaflet with the headline, "Charity Begins at Home: The shocking story of the Montefiore hospital workers." The text compared the low wages of Montefiore workers, some of whom worked full-time and yet were eligible for welfare, with the higher wages of city employees doing similar work.

The NLRB gives employees the right to vote in a representation election once a union signs up 30 percent of the workers in a bargaining unit. But since hospitals weren't covered under the NLRB, we were sure that no matter how many signed cards we got, management would ignore us. We thought we'd eventually have to strike for recognition. So Godoff was always testing to see if the workers would stick their necks out. We didn't want to head into a strike with workers who weren't ready.

One strategy came from my memories of the student movement. I suggested in 1958 that we make a giant telegram like one we'd made twenty years earlier supporting Republican Spain during the Spanish Civil War. We hung the telegram outside the hospital. It was maybe twenty feet across and said in big lettering: "To Mr. Victor Riesenfeld, President, Montefiore Board of Directors. We the undersigned have a right to a union."

Asking people to put their names on it was a test, and hundreds of workers signed. Then Godoff would organize demonstrations outside the hospital after work from 4 to 6 P.M. If you were willing to walk around with a sign asking for union recognition, that meant something. Then Godoff would say, "Now let's do it at lunch time, where they'll have to go outside and come back in." He was always testing.

The only staffers seriously involved in the yearlong campaign were Godoff, Mitchell, Davis, and myself, and of course Dave and I had lots of other responsibilities. We would have gotten nowhere without a strong committee of Montefiore workers.

We had close to a majority signed up when I went to Davis and said, "What we're doing is good, but we can't beat Montefiore without public support."

"That's a good idea," he said. "Get it."

"I don't know what to do," I said.

"Figure it out," he answered.

So I picked up the phone and started calling reporters and potential community allies. An initial problem was convincing people there still were workers in New York making thirty dollars a week. "Don't kid me," they'd say. "There's a minimum wage." Sometimes they'd hang up before I could tell them hospital workers were exempt from the minimum wage law.

The first papers I interested were the *Amsterdam News*, a black-run weekly with offices in Harlem, and *El Diario*, a Spanish daily. I went to the office of *Amsterdam News* publisher James Hicks with

Mitchell and a delegation of workers holding their pay stubs, and Hicks wrote an editorial about injustice at Montefiore. I started using the phrase "forgotten men and women" and asked *El Diario* to write about them, and *El Diario* did.

The mainstream press was harder. My first opening was through James Wechsler, editor of the *New York Post*. He was a thoroughly decent guy and became a crucial ally. He listened to my first phone call and said, "Have you spoken to Mrs. Roosevelt?"

"How am I going to do that?" I asked.

By the end of the day I was meeting with her. Eleanor Roosevelt, widow of President Franklin Roosevelt, was a tremendously respected voice for the underdog. She took up our cause in her "My Day" column in the *World Telegram and Sun*. And Wechsler began writing columns and editorials about us.

Then Max Steinbock, editor of the paper at our international union, the Retail, Wholesale and Department Store Union (RWDSU), suggested I talk to Evans Clark, a member of the *New York Times* editorial board. Clark printed a letter to the editor from Davis demanding Montefiore recognize the union, but nothing happened. I called Clark and asked for an editorial.

"Absolutely not," he said. "We write editorials about whole industries—steel, railroad, auto. We don't write editorials about a single hospital."

But I kept calling, presenting it as a battle of good versus evil. One day he said, "Give me a little bit more of the facts."

Then he wrote an editorial November 21, 1958, asking:

> Isn't it unfair and inhuman to ask hospital workers to help meet hospital deficits by accepting substandard wages? Shouldn't voluntary hospital managements deal with unions that represent a majority of their employees—even though no state law compels them to? Shouldn't wages be raised to at least city hospital levels? Shouldn't the state bring hospital employees under the provisions of state labor laws?

That was a bombshell. Also, by this time the *Post* had printed three editorials. The hospitals used to call the *Post* the downtown edition of *1199 News*. It was a very different paper back then. With all that publicity, people were looking around and saying, "What the hell is going on?"

As a result of this campaign, the American Public Relations Association in 1958 gave me its annual Silver Anvil award for "outstanding public relations performance." It was the only time before or since that the award was given to a labor union.

We were moving in other areas also. Davis and I had gone to see Harry Van Arsdale, president of the New York City Central Labor Council. The Council represented unions with more than two million members, and Van Arsdale was close to New York Mayor Robert Wagner. Van Arsdale liked the idea of uniting labor in a campaign for poor and nonwhite people, and he became a key ally.

We had involved some black and Hispanic leaders by this time. Dr. King's important New York advisor Bayard Rustin supported us, as did leaders such as state legislator Emilio Nunez and Herman Badillo, who later served in Congress and headed the board of the City University of New York.

Meanwhile, I found out that Montefiore's public relations man, Victor Weingarten, was a guy you could talk to. He told us the trustees were very concerned about their growing PR problem. They were also under tremendous pressure not to give in from the rest of the hospitals, who didn't want a precedent set. But there was a liberal faction on Montefiore's board, and the votes on union recognition were getting closer.

A turning point came November 28, 1958, when Davis wrote Montefiore's CEO, Dr. Martin Cherkasky, a personal letter appealing to Cherkasky's better instincts. Davis had discovered that Cherkasky had a history of concern for social justice. In his letter, Davis said Montefiore might be able to destroy the union if it wished. But, he asked, would that "solve any problems for the management, for the workers, or for you who must assume a great share of the burden?"

Looking back, Cherkasky called the letter the "final blow. There wasn't a chord in me that Leon didn't strike." The two men continued a friendly relationship of mutual respect until Davis's death in 1992.

At about the same time as the letter to Cherkasky, Weingarten called and told me a crucial trustees vote was coming up. He said one more *Times* editorial might do the trick. I called Clark. The following morning a *Times* editorial said Montefiore had a public responsibility to avoid a strike over union recognition and that the trustees should agree to an election.

Montefiore agreed. The election was held December 30, 1958. The workers voted 628 to 31 for 1199 representation.

The celebration at our Montefiore headquarters up on Gun Hill Road was like the second coming. The workers felt such great happiness. For me, it was like we had beaten the odds, like my boyhood fictional hero Frank Merriwell doing the impossible. And the interesting thing was, we were just feeling our way, learning the ropes. We had some gifted people who could dig a ditch, and from every ditch we made a trench. Back then, we could work from early morning until late at night, and everybody was excited. It was inspiring.

By March 1959 we had a contract at Montefiore providing a thirty dollar-per-month pay increase, time-and-a-half after forty hours a week, a grievance procedure, and sick leave and vacation time.

One Saturday, Cherkasky asked Davis and me to bring the contract to his office so he could sign it. Afterward he pointed to me and asked Dave, "What do you pay this guy?"

Dave said, "Seventy-five dollars a week."

"You have a good buy," said Cherkasky.

News about Montefiore spread around the city like wildfire. Workers were calling and saying, "We want to join the union from Montefiore." We distributed thousands of application cards and the postman was carrying in stacks and stacks of returns. Godoff started making charts of hospital departments where we had strength, and it was growing daily. In different corners of our headquarters there would be meetings every night of workers from various hospitals. We didn't even know where some of the hospitals were. We took the drugstore organizers off their regular assignments and sent them out to the hospitals to organize. We sent Montefiore members all around the city to speak. A revolution was underway.

Another thing happening was that contact with the workers was making our staff more determined. A lot of us who had been in the Left were opposed to racism on principle, but we didn't know a whole lot of the details. I remember meeting an active African American union supporter at Knickerbocker Hospital (it doesn't exist anymore) in Harlem.

"I want to be able to write something about you in *1199 News*. I want to know more," I said to her. "Could I come to your home?"

She ducked me for a long time, but finally she agreed. Her apartment and the details of her life shocked me. I could tell she kept the place clean. But the paint was peeling. The furniture was shabby. The children's clothes were worn. She made twenty-eight dollars a week for full-time work and was on supplementary welfare.

I never forgot it. I was enraged, and I directed that rage at the hospitals, which I regarded as responsible. And I think a lot of our staff had similar experiences. From then on, I made everything into an issue of good versus evil. That feeling made me determined not to give up. It made me want to get people's attention, to grab them by the collar if I had to, but to somehow get them to see that something was wrong. And I wanted to get across the attitude, "How can you possibly go home tonight without doing something about it?"

Many of our drugstore members felt the same way. We relied heavily on the Crack of Dawn Brigades—the name we gave to the hundreds of drugstore members who joined in organizing hospitals. They'd come to union headquarters at night to pick up leaflets and then get up before dawn and spend an hour or two handing them out at hospitals before continuing on to their drugstore jobs. They'd start leafleting around 5:30 A.M. because hospital workers come to work early.

In addition to the more active members who joined the Crack of Dawn Brigades, the entire 1199 membership voted to increase their dues by a dollar a month to support the hospital organizing drive. The dedication of these members, mostly Jewish men, in supporting the fight of mostly minority women hospital workers continued the 1199 tradition of member activism and working-class solidarity. It was a major factor in the organizing drive and in the 1959 strike that followed.

Davis expanded the full-time paid hospital organizing team by adding Godoff's old ally Marshall Dubin, Montefiore licensed practical nurse (LPN) Thelma Bowles, and Jesse Olson, a pharmacist and active delegate who took a sixty-five-dollar a week pay cut to join the staff. Olson later rose to become an 1199 executive vice president and head of the union's important Guild of Technical, Professional, Office and Clerical Employees.

Support from other unions started building after the Montefiore victory. District 65 gave us ten organizers and some money. Van Arsdale remained with us.

Our 1959 campaign coincided with the early days of the civil rights movement in the South. The Montgomery bus boycott had already happened, and Dr. King had become a national figure. I was friendly with Stanley Levison, a New York lawyer who was a close advisor to Dr. King and King's lieutenant, Andrew Young. Levison got me a meeting with King. We told him what we were doing.

"This is great. Count me in," King said. "Whatever I can do, call on me. Deal through Stanley for anything you want from me."

So I'd call Stanley and say, "I need a statement over Dr. King's name," or "Can we publicize Dr. King's backing on this subject?" Being able to say that Dr. King supported 1199 at such-and-such a hospital became a powerful tool.

Coverage in the Hispanic and black press was extensive. They were taking credit for what was happening. Sometimes they printed my news releases word for word or even let me write editorials that said things like "*El Diario* is proud to have been among the first to join the crusade of the hospital workers." *La crusada*, that's what we called it. Dan Wakefield covered us in *The Nation* magazine in an article titled "Victims of Charity." He later did a wonderful piece in *Dissent* magazine. A lot of the reporters were emotionally moved by the workers they met, by their determination to get out of poverty.

As we grew stronger, management launched a counteroffensive led by the Greater New York Hospital Association. They felt Montefiore had been weak with us, but that the other hospitals could resist. Stories began appearing about how unions in hospitals would be disastrous to patients—workers wouldn't do their jobs and service would be interrupted by strikes. We argued that most hospital strikes were for recognition because management wouldn't agree to elections, but of course that didn't stop them.

Some hospitals became more repressive. For instance, Knickerbocker Hospital demanded that all employees talk English on the job because they feared workers were talking union in Spanish. Workers around the city were fired for union activity.

By the spring of 1959, we decided to focus on a few hospitals where we had the greatest majorities. These were Mount Sinai, Beth Israel, Beth David (now closed), and Lenox Hill in Manhattan; Bronx (now Bronx Lebanon); and Brooklyn Jewish (now Interfaith). Since all of these but Lenox Hill were endowed by the Federation of Jewish Philanthropies, some people said we were intentionally picking on Jewish hospitals. That wasn't true. We just looked at the numbers and went where we were strongest. The fact that most of these places were Jewish may have been because workers at the Catholic hospitals were more frightened and the big Protestant institutions like Presbyterian, St. Luke's, and New York Hospitals were richer and paid a little more.

We asked for elections. Management stonewalled. In late March we had a strike vote. We explained to the workers that a strike might be long and difficult, that the union had no money to pay strike benefits, and that there might be injunctions and jail sentences. But we said that if members went to jail, leaders would too. The vote was 2,258 to 95 to strike.

The city got into the act and proposed third-party fact finding. Management refused. We didn't want a strike and were doing what we could to avoid it. We got the *Times* and the *Post* and Mrs. Roosevelt to call for management to sit down with us. Van Arsdale set up meetings at City Hall. But management refused to sit in the same room with Leon Davis. They said that would mean tacit union recognition.

The night before May 8, when the strike began, is very clear in my memory. The officers and staff spent the whole night in the conference room at union headquarters, which then occupied two floors at 709 Eighth Avenue on the corner of 45th Street. There were less than

Brooklyn College basketball team, 1934. Foner standing second from right. He's not in uniform because he had to leave immediately after photo session for band date.

Suspended Swing (the Foners' band name), 1941, at Arrowhead Lodge in Ellenville, N.Y. *Left to right:* Jack Foner, drums; Hal Schor, piano; Everett Birch, trumpet; Moe Foner, tenor saxophone; Henry Foner, alto saxophone; and Norman Franklin, alto saxophone.

Foner outside District 65 headquarters at 13 Astor Place in Manhattan with car he drove from August 1949 Peekskill, N.Y. Robeson riot. He holds one of the rocks that were thrown through his car windows. None of the car occupants were seriously hurt.

Meeting in 1947 of production staff and advisory committee for "Thursdays 'Til Nine," musical comedy produced by Department Store Employees Union. *Clockwise from left:* Co-author Norman Franklin, lighting director Peggy Clark, advisor Norman Rosten, producer Moe Foner, co-author Henry Foner, musical director Robert Lenn, advisors Millard Lampell and Martin Ritt, and choreographers Muriel Mannings and William Korff. (Courtesy 1199)

Mary and Abe Foner, 1950s. He died in 1959. She died in 1967.

Eleanor Roosevelt at 1199 in 1950s. She appeared at 1199 Teen Time events organized by Foner and later supported 1199's 1959 hospital strike. *Left to right:* 1199 president Leon Davis, Mrs. Roosevelt, 1199 officers William J. Taylor and Edward Ayash, and Foner. (Courtesy 1199)

Foner and 1199 president Leon Davis in Davis's office in union headquarters at Eighth Ave. and 45th St. in Manhattan during 1959 hospital strike. (Courtesy 1199)

Scene on Mount Sinai Hospital picket line during 1959 strike. (Courtesy 1199)

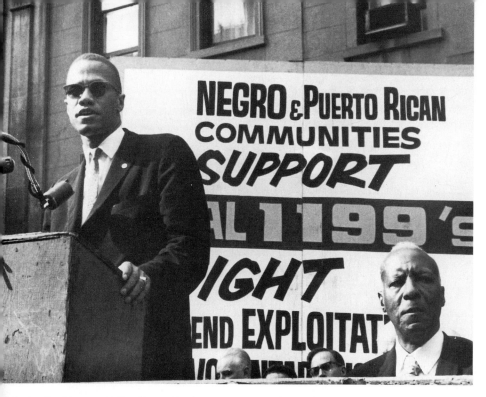

Malcolm X addresses 1962 rally on Manhattan's West 72nd St. in support of 1199 hospital strike. At right is sleeping car porter's union president and civil rights leader A. Philip Randolph. It was the only time Malcolm X ever spoke in support of a labor union. (Courtesy 1199)

Governor Nelson Rockefeller in 1963 signed bill extending collective bargaining rights to workers in voluntary hospitals in New York City. *Left to right:* Leon Davis, Rockefeller, Foner, and 1199 officers Elliott Godoff and Doris Turner. (Courtesy 1199)

1199 strike in 1965 a
Lawrence Hospital ir
Bronxville, N.Y., led to col
lective bargaining rights for
hospital workers throughou
New York State. Walking
toward camera in hat i
Ossie Davis. (New York'
Health and Human Servic
Union, 1199/SEIU Archives
Kheel Center, Corne
University

Dr. King at February 1968
1199 Salute to Freedom with
1199 officer Henry Nicholas.
(Courtesy Miller Photography)

Historic contract victory in 1968 brought 1199 hospital workers a one-hundred-dollar-a-week minimum wage and major benefit improvements. (New York's Health and Human Service Union, 1199/SEIU Archives, Kheel Center, Cornell University)

1199 strike at two Charleston, S.C., hospitals in 1969 united labor and civil rights movements and captured national attention. The four hundred workers involved were almost all black women. Some are shown here at strike rally in a Charleston church. (Courtesy 1199)

Foner with the Reverend Andrew Young, Southern Christian Leadership Conference executive vice president, during May 1969 Mothers Day March of Charleston strikers. (Courtesy 1199)

After Charleston, Mrs. King traveled to many cities to support 1199 hospital organizing drives. She's shown here with Foner in 1969 outside Johns Hopkins Hospital in Baltimore. Workers there voted to join Local 1199E that year. (Courtesy 1199)

National Hospital Union founding convention in 1973 heard (left to right) New York City Central Labor Council president Harry Van Arsdale, United Farm Workers president Cesar Chavez, Coretta King, and 1199 president Leon Davis. (Courtesy 1199)

Foner holds up 1973 newspaper's "Complete List of White House's Enemies," which contained his name. Foner said he was proud to have made President Nixon's Enemies List and promised to justify the president's confidence in him. (New York's Health and Human Service Union, 1199/SEIU Archives, Kheel Center, Cornell University)

1199 was an early opponent of Vietnam War. Foner was national coordinator of Labor Leadership Assembly for Peace. 1199ers turned out in force for all major anti-Vietnam War demonstrations of the 1960s and 1970s, including this one in Washington, D.C. (New York's Health and Human Service Union, 1199/SEIU Archives, Kheel Center, Cornell University)

1199ers struck League of Voluntary Hospital of Greater New York in 1976 for higher wages. Members are at rally at City Hall.(New York's Health and Human Service Union, 1199/SEIU Archives, Kheel Center, Cornell University)

Jane Fonda appeared with Foner in 1979 at press conference at Gallery 1199 at union's New York headquarters. Fonda read James Oppenheim's poem "Bread and Roses," which is based on 1912 strike of textile workers in Lawrence, Massachusetts. Bread and Roses conducted series of events commemorating Lawrence strike. (Courtesy 1199)

Stanley Levison, a key advisor to Dr. King and a friend of 1199, died September 12, 1979. Singing "We Shall Overcome" at his memorial were, left to right, Levison's son Andrew, Coretta King, Foner, the Reverend Andrew Young, and former U.S. Attorney General Ramsey Clark. (Courtesy 1199)

Harry Belafonte's first New York City performance in seventeen years came in 1980 at an 1199 Bread and Roses concert that sold out Lincoln Center's Avery Fisher Hall. Foner and Belafonte are shown here. Belafonte told the 2,800 1199ers in the audience that he was proud to have walked many 1199 picket lines. (Courtesy Miller Photography)

Foner with New York City Central Labor Council president Harry Van Arsdale on occasion of 1982 Distinguished Service Award to Foner from the Council, which represented unions with two million members. (New York's Health and Human Service Union, 1199/SEIU Archives, Kheel Center, Cornell University)

1199 Bread and Roses Labor Day Street Fairs drew tens of thousands to varied programs. Foner is shown here at 1981 fair with John Sweeney, then president of the Service Employees International Union and later president of the AFL-CIO. (Courtesy 1199)

Foner with Harry Belafonte in 1987 at Gallery 1199 photo exhibition "King Remembered." (Courtesy 1199)

Foner with wife Anne in 1989 following Foner's hip replacement surgery. (Courtesy Miller Photography)

The late John Cardinal O'Connor, Roman Catholic archbishop of New York, was a staunch supporter of labor. He supported 1199's drive to organize low-paid home care workers. Hundreds of 1199ers attended his annual Labor Masses at St. Patrick's Cathedral. He's shown here wearing an 1199 hat at a 1990 Labor Day Parade. (Courtesy 1199)

Leon Davis died September 14, 1992, at the age of eighty-four. Speakers at an October 5 memorial meeting at Lincoln Center's Avery Fisher Hall organized and chaired by Foner are shown here. Foner is second from left, standing next to 1199 president Dennis Rivera. (Courtesy Miller Photography)

Foner with Dennis Rivera (center) and Ossie Davis at 1994 Labor Research Association annual dinner at which Foner received Lifetime Achievement Award "for his leadership in promoting the culture of working people." (Courtesy 1199)

Foner with Dennis Rivera (left) and Service Employees International Union president Andrew Stern a the opening in Gallery 1199 of one of a series of touring student art exhibits organized by Bread and Roses in the late 1990s. Topics included "Working," "Sweatshops," and "Why Unions Matter." (Courtesy 1199)

Foner receives honorary Doctor of Fine Arts in May 2000 from New School University's Parsons School of Design at commencement ceremony at Riverside Church in upper Manhattan. Chancellor Philip Scaturro, in presenting the degree, said: "Your vision is egalitarian; everyone, regardless of class, origin, or formal education, deserves the opportunity to reflect on the meaning of their lives. Exposure to the arts, you realized, was no one's exclusive domain. You boldly launched Bread and Roses to bring the arts directly to the workplace." (Courtesy 1199)

twenty of us. Talks at City Hall had broken down during the evening. I napped with my head on the table. At 5 A.M. Davis said, "Okay, the strike starts at six. Everybody to the hospital where you're assigned." Everybody went out but Dave and me. I stayed to talk to the press. And I remember feeling we had no idea what would happen.

We were feeling aggressive, that we were fighting the good fight. But would the workers come out? That was the question.

And then we got reports, this many people crossed the line here, this many there, and we realized that it was a small number and that the workers were with us. The next realization was, now we have to really do it, we must continue this fight against powerful forces.

Another question was Van Arsdale. He had said we had Central Labor Council support for everything up to a strike. But he warned us not to go out. Then, as we approached May 8, the hospitals' arrogance infuriated him, and he eventually became an enthusiastic part of our strike leadership.

MOUNT Sinai, Beth Israel, Beth David, Bronx, Brooklyn Jewish, and Lenox Hill Hospitals walked out May 8. They stayed out forty-six days, which is more than six weeks and felt like forever. On June 5 the workers struck at Flower and Fifth Ave. Hospital, a Manhattan institution that closed many years later. The total number of strikers was about 3,500.

We had made strike preparations, but we'd never been in anything as big as this, and we learned the ropes as we went along. Hospitals function twenty-four hours a day, so we needed picket lines up all the time to prevent workers from going in. This involved detailed organization, with committees and strike captains to ensure participation was at a maximum and hardship reduced wherever possible. We had picket duty committees, food committees, publicity committees, all sorts of committees at each hospital. We put out a daily strike bulletin to keep the workers informed. The spirit of the strikers was amazing. It was like they'd been freed after lifetimes of being bottled up. When their morale needed bolstering, we had folksingers like Pete Seeger and Joe Glazer at the picket lines leading them in union songs.

There were numerous picket line brawls with the cops and arrests by the hundreds. At Flower and Fifth, one hundred strikers decided to join an academic procession that was part of the New York Medical College graduation. Many were beaten with nightsticks and seven were arrested. A police spokesman called it "the worst picket line violence in ten years." There was plenty of coverage of that incident.

We didn't have strike benefits, but we did have strike kitchens outside each hospital. Other unions took on the job of providing food. The bakery workers would bring bread, cakes, and rolls every day. The Amalgamated Meat Cutters and Butcher Workmen provided two weeks' worth of meat to every striker plus thousands of pounds of cold cuts to strike headquarters. The International Union of Electrical Workers delivered 48,000 eggs and 4,000 chickens. The Transport Workers Union, whose president, Mike Quill, called the hospital trustees worse than Arkansas's racist governor, Orville Faubus, in their treatment of black strikers, donated thousands of cans of food and picket line support.

Davis's wife Julia had been a social worker, and she began an assistance program, helping strikers with needs like housing, rent, or late payment of bills.

The committee in charge of strike operations consisted of Davis, Godoff, myself, and Bill Taylor, a former drugstore soda man who was then a vice president and later became secretary treasurer and head of the union's Benefit and Pension Funds.

My job was mostly dealing with the press and building community support. Obviously, it would have been a disaster if the public simply associated us with neglecting the sick. Instead, we wanted our members to be seen for what they were: dedicated workers who were terribly underpaid. We pointed out that management, not exploited workers, should be blamed for labor unrest. Our theme was that the workers were involuntary philanthropists, compelled to subsidize hospital deficits through substandard wages. I came up with the slogan "Be Fair to Those Who Care." We've used this slogan ever since on our picket signs, leaflets, and elsewhere.

I worked closely with Davis during the strike, but that was sometimes complicated. Injunctions were issued, and Davis was often "in hiding" to avoid being served a subpoena. That usually meant staying in a hotel room where we would telephone him. But sometimes he'd come back to the office and work at his own desk. We just wouldn't tell anyone he was there.

After the first two weeks we realized that because we hadn't organized the technical and professional workers, the strike couldn't be fully effective. The hospitals could get by with supervisors and society volunteers doing the service jobs. One volunteer came to the hospital with her butler. Channel 2 interviewed her outside the hospital. When they asked about the butler, she said:

"Well, he does everything for me at home, so I thought he would come and do everything here too."

Management remained determined not to give in. It was a standoff. So the press and support from civil rights, labor, religious, and political sources became even more important. That was my job.

We formed a Committee for Justice to Hospital Workers. It was headed by Sleeping Car Porters president and long-time civil rights leader A. Philip Randolph, Puerto Rican leader Joseph Monserrat, and theologian Reinhold Niebuhr. We had backing from people like Eleanor Roosevelt, the American Civil Liberties Union (ACLU), former U.S. Senator Herbert Lehman, the Association of Reform Rabbis, the Protestant Council of New York City, Congressmen Adam Clayton Powell and Emanuel Celler, psychologist Kenneth Clark, and City Councilman Stanley Isaacs.

Powell, who was also pastor of the Abyssinian Baptist Church, maybe the most important black church in the city, brought his congregation down to join the Mount Sinai picket line one Sunday after services. That made headlines and television.

We had already linked ourselves with the young civil rights movement, stressing that we were in a struggle for union and human rights. We got a statement from Dr. King saying that the hospital struggle was against degradation, poverty, and misery, that it was against all the evils that afflict poor black people in this society. We used that statement over and over. Bayard Rustin worked closely with us to build support in the black community.

It was summer and without competing news, the press gave us a big play. Most of it was supportive. I remember *Times* Pulitzer Prize winner Homer Bigart. He was a Pittsburgh Pirates fan and was always trying to get their games on a little transistor radio. He called me one Saturday and said, "Moe, we need a good Sunday peg to get on the front page. How about you give me a statement that management is aiming this strike at poor blacks and polarizing the city?"

I said, "Sure."

He said, "Now I'll go to Buttonwieser."

Benjamin Buttonwieser was chairman of the board at Lenox Hill and a socially prominent hardnose who stopped donating to the Urban League when the League supported the right of hospital workers to an election.

Buttonwieser gave Bigart an angry statement of denial, and Bigart had his story.

Gabe Pressman and Mike Wallace covered the strike, and Jimmy Wechsler made sure the *Post*'s coverage was good, despite pressure on the publisher, Dorothy Schiff, from her hospital trustee friends.

The *Times* didn't take permanent sides. At first it said the strike was immoral. Then it began calling for a settlement and for state legislation to give hospital workers the right to representation elections. That was pretty good considering that Mount Sinai board member Alfred Rose walked to work every morning with *Times* publisher Arthur Hays Sulzberger.

The *Post* columnist Murray Kempton called the strike "the most clear-cut social issue since the revolt of the gladiators." And later, in the *New York Review of Books*, he mentioned 1199, "whose strikes have become known around the country as wars of national liberation."

Mayor Wagner had to show he was involved, so for most of the strike he had meetings with both sides where nothing happened. Management would sit in one room and labor, led by Van Arsdale, in another. Van Arsdale said Wagner had one bad ear and whenever he'd heard enough he'd turn his head and let you talk into it. That happened a lot.

The support Van Arsdale organized from the rest of the labor movement and the role he played with the politicians was really something. There would be no 1199 if it weren't for Harry Van Arsdale.

Besides the food he organized from the other unions there were major financial contributions. The largest came from Van Arsdale's own union, Local 3 of the International Brotherhood of Electrical Workers.

Halfway through the strike, the *Journal American*, the Hearst paper, came out with a front-page story headlined, "The Communist Past of the Strike Leaders." It talked almost entirely about Davis. Most of our members didn't know a Communist from a hole in the ground. They didn't care. But it was a problem with some of the union heads Van Arsdale had to deal with.

Van Arsdale called me and said, "I need a statement from Davis by tomorrow morning saying he's not a Communist."

Davis wrote the statement, and Van Arsdale read it the next morning to the executive board of the Central Labor Council. When he asked for questions there were none.

"Okay," he said. "The question is closed. I don't want to hear it any more."

That was the end of that as a strike issue.

Van Arsdale used to ride around to the picket lines every day on a motorcycle. He'd raise the strikers' spirits and he'd get invigorated himself. I was there once when he called AFL-CIO Pres. George Meany:

"George, it would do your heart good to come down here," Van Arsdale told Meany, who used to boast he'd never walked a picket line.

Harry thought he'd get Meany on our line, but that didn't happen. Meany did support the strike, though.

Somewhere in the middle of the strike Van Arsdale said to me, "This is a strike we should make a film about. You should do it."

"Sure," I said.

But I put it off. We were in over our heads, going without sleep, and I couldn't see taking on anything else.

Every time I'd see him, Harry would say, "How's the film coming?" or "Don't forget about the film." Finally he started saying he needed it to show at a big Central Labor Council meeting in October.

I knew I had to do something, so I called Faith Hubley. I'd met her through my theatrical friends. She and her husband, John, had originated "Mr. Magoo" and won Academy Awards for their animated films.

"Faith, I've got this problem and I don't know what to do," I said.

"Okay," she said. "You come to my apartment on Fifth Ave. at 5 P.M. next Tuesday. I'm going to have a cocktail party. I'll invite filmmakers and you be prepared to talk about the strike."

There must have been one hundred filmmakers there. On the spot they raised fifteen hundred dollars for the strikers. Then Faith told them she and her husband couldn't make a film about the strike because of other commitments, but were there any volunteers? Two people raised their hands. One was John Schultz, a CBS-TV editor who had worked with Edward R. Murrow on *Harvest of Shame*. The other was Pat Jaffe, also a skilled filmmaker. Within a month, using TV footage and interviews with strikers, they made a film, *Hospital Strike*. I wrote the script and Ossie Davis narrated it. Tony Schwartz, a radio sound expert, did the sound. The movie was very effective. Our members loved it, and Van Arsdale got to show it in October as scheduled.

One day in the middle of June, Van Arsdale met with Davis and me in a darkened hotel room where Davis was in hiding.

"I think we've gone about as far as we can go," Harry said. "I don't think we can keep it up much longer, and I don't think there's much we can get."

He described what management was about to offer at City Hall. It included establishment of a permanent administrative committee made up of twelve representatives from the hospitals and the public (but not the union) to make annual recommendations on wages and working conditions. Wages would immediately improve to a forty dollar a week minimum (one dollar an hour), with paid overtime, for many almost a ten dollar weekly raise. The committee would allow arbitration, but the union wouldn't be permitted to appear until the final step in the arbitration process, outside the hospital. All the strikers would be allowed to return to work with no reprisals. Workers could join the union and elect representatives if they wished, but the hospitals wouldn't recognize the union, and organizers would not be allowed inside.

"It's bad, but I don't think we can go any further," said Van Arsdale. "We have a meeting tonight at City Hall. Let me know."

Davis called Godoff over to the hotel. We understood that management's offer was not very different from what they had offered before the strike.

"Elliott, can we live with it?" said Davis.

"I think we might have a chance," Godoff said. "We'll have to because we can't go any further without the AFL-CIO."

Davis agreed with him. Godoff thought a little bit and added:

"The important thing is with no reprisals we can all go back to work together. We'll try to keep the union alive that way. The spirit of the workers, that's what counts. If we can keep that spirit up at the settlement meeting, that will help. We have to talk positively."

When I heard that I started working on a plan.

Davis scheduled a membership meeting for Monday, June 22, at the Diplomat Hotel in midtown Manhattan for the strikers to vote on the settlement proposal. Van Arsdale had insisted to me that nothing be released to the press until after the workers met. I called Davis on the Saturday before the meeting and said:

"Dave, you don't have to assume responsibility for this. I'll be responsible, and you don't know anything about it. I'm going to start calling reporters."

My idea was to begin getting a positive spin as early as possible.

First I called Jimmy Wechsler at the *Post* and Evans Clark at the *Times*. They agreed to do what they could. Then I called the *Times* labor reporter Stanley Levey, Jack Turcott at the *Daily News* and wire service, and television and radio people. I told them the same story, which was nothing, in a sense, but everything in another sense.

I alerted them to an important membership meeting Monday night. I knew they were all going to ask if it was about a settlement and what was in the settlement.

"I can't tell you what the workers will be voting on, I'm forbidden," I said. "But remember the fact-finding committee report a couple of weeks ago? If you read that you'll know pretty much what the settlement proposal is."

Mayor Wagner had appointed a fact-finding committee in May headed by prominent mediator William H. Davis. The panel's June 8 recommendations closely resembled management's final offer except that the panel came a little nearer to union recognition by allowing thinly veiled union representatives into the grievance procedure. Management didn't like that and rejected the recommendation.

The important thing was that we had waited until management's rejection and then approved the panel's proposal. I reminded the reporters of that. They got the idea, and their stories Monday morning all mentioned that although the details of the settlement proposal were not known, they had earlier been rejected by management and accepted by the union. Then they went on to give the details of the William H. Davis panel's proposal.

And that became the settlement terms in the minds of the strikers and the public. The membership meeting June 22 was a victory rally. Television showed the workers carrying Davis and Van Arsdale around on their shoulders. There were one thousand strikers there, and I think there was one "No" vote. We had turned defeat into victory.

I wasn't there. My daughter Nancy was graduating from junior high school that night, and my wife insisted I be there. I told Dave and he said, "I'm ordering you to go to the graduation."

Later that night I saw Dave interviewed on television.

"But you didn't win real union recognition, Mr. Davis," said the interviewer.

"No, we didn't," Dave answered. "We won backdoor recognition. But we'll be in the front door soon."

And that's just what happened.

4. Like a Beautiful Child

The Hospital Union Comes of Age

MANAGEMENT THOUGHT the Permanent Administrative Committee created in the 1959 strike settlement would give workers some gains while ignoring 1199, and that gradually the hospital union would shrivel and die. That strategy overlooked two factors.

First, it overlooked the mood of the workers. Going back to their jobs with some actual gains electrified the strikers. They felt that finally they had spoken up; they had been heard by the whole city, and they had survived. The union became like a church to them. It was something they believed in deeply. It was theirs. It was their way to a better life. And like a church, it provided the setting for some very capable people to emerge as leaders.

Some of these leaders remained at their hospital jobs for many years, strengthening the union as solid delegates. Among them were Mount Sinai laundry worker Gloria Arana and Beth Israel housekeeper Hilda Joquin. Joquin stood less than five feet tall, but she packed a wallop. She became famous for outwitting a supervisor who told her he'd fire her if she wore her union button on her hospital-issued uniform. She stared him right in the eye, took the button off her lapel, and pinned it in her hair.

Other 1959 strikers joined the union staff, some climbing to important leadership positions. Henry Nicholas, a former Mount Sinai orderly who became Godoff's right-hand man, succeeded Davis as

National Hospital Union president, and now heads AFSCME's national hospital division. Doris Turner, a former Lenox Hill dietary clerk who headed 1199's Hospital Division for nearly two decades, succeeded Davis as president of 1199 in New York from 1982 to 1986. Ramon Malave moved from the Beth Israel storeroom to become an 1199 vice president. Bronx Hospital maintenance man Joe Brown became an organizer in the Bronx and head of 1199's softball league. Everybody called him "Commissioner." Former Mount Sinai orderly Julio Pagan worked in Godoff's organizing department and brought in many hundreds of new members. Longtime Beth David worker Maria Munoz joined the staff as an organizer.

They were just a few of the many strikers who went on to bring racial, ethnic, and gender diversity to 1199's staff and leadership. Organizers and officers like them provided firsthand experience when union leaders talked about the problems and hopes of hospital workers.

The second factor overlooked by hospital management in 1959 was the ingenuity and perseverance of the union, which regarded the Permanent Administrative Committee as a brief stop on the way to real recognition.

Our strategy after the 1959 strike was to achieve organized power in the workplace and enough political power to win passage in Albany of collective bargaining rights.

To organize power in the hospitals, we started collecting dues of three dollars a month so we could pay organizers. We trained delegates to collect dues, handle grievances, and spread the union message. We set up a structure of delegates, chapters at each hospital, and delegate assemblies. And Godoff came up with a couple of dramatic actions that caught people's imaginations.

One was the "high noon." This started as an organizing technique in which workers demanded union recognition. But after a while we did it all the time. Whenever we could bring together a decent number of members around a local issue, their delegates would lead them at 12 noon into the executive director's office. They'd crowd in and state their case until they got some kind of a satisfactory response.

Another event was the mock funeral at Brooklyn Jewish. Management demonstrated its meanness by offering thirty-two-dollar-a-week workers a two-cents-an-hour raise. The workers rejected the increase and staged a funeral for it on the hospital steps, complete with a coffin, pall bearers, wax flowers, and crocodile tears.

The workers loved this kind of thing. We got stronger in our hospital base and developed considerable new strength in additional hospitals around the city. At a now-closed Manhattan hospital called Trafalgar, we actually got a contract.

A problem that has plagued us for decades emerged during this period. Certain other unions, sensing that organizing health care workers might be the wave of the future, went to managements and offered themselves as a more agreeable alternative than 1199. Some actually got contracts this way. This led to some bitter fights with one union in particular until we made a "Column A–Column B" agreement that sketched out separate territories for the two unions.

Winning collective bargaining rights through changing the state law was a different story. We recognized that we'd get nowhere until this happened. So when the state legislature began its 1960 session, I went to Albany to start a campaign. It took five years. We started by bringing big delegations of members to the Capitol to lobby. We got support from liberal organizations and legislators and groups like the National Association for the Advancement of Colored People (NAACP). The assembly passed the labor law amendment we wanted in 1961, but it died in the Senate. That taught us that to get anywhere we'd have to get action from Gov. Nelson Rockefeller, a Republican, and to get action from Rockefeller we'd have to make something happen.

That something was another strike. One of our organizing targets was Beth El (now Brookdale) Hospital in Brooklyn. When Beth El refused to give us an election in the spring of 1962, we struck for recognition. That strike lasted fifty-six days. Somewhere in the middle of it we added Manhattan Eye, Ear and Throat Hospital. The strike was in many ways a replay of 1959.

An injunction was issued against us, and this time Leon Davis went to jail for thirty days, during which time he fasted. When he came out he refused to call off the strike and faced sentencing to six months.

We had a street rally on the East Side that was the only time Malcolm X gave public support to a union. He praised Davis for going to jail and told the crowd, "If you aren't willing to pay the price, then you don't need the rewards or benefits that go along with it." Other speakers at the rally included A. Philip Randolph, NAACP Executive Director Roy Wilkins, and socialist leader Norman Thomas.

We even got a progressive Beth El trustee to publicly resign from the board in indignation over the trustees' disregard for union and human rights. He was rich and had a pavilion at the hospital named after him. At the last minute, he got cold feet and almost changed his mind.

"Do you think they'll take my name off the pavilion marquee if I withdraw from the board?" he asked us.

There were picket line incidents and hundreds of arrests. We had liberal support and favorable editorials, but the hospitals didn't budge.

I had become friendly with Hank Paley, the key aide to the Republican Speaker of the Assembly, Joseph Carlino. Through Paley, Carlino had become an ally and was talking to Governor Rockefeller. We were fortunate that it was a gubernatorial election year.

In early July, Paley, Solomon L. Corbin (the governor's counsel), and I met for lunch at the Hotel Manhattan to discuss possible ways to end the strike. I suggested a solution I thought they'd like because it would make the governor look like a hero. The idea was that Rockefeller would make a campaign pledge to support our legislation as a condition for ending the strike.

The problem was how Rockefeller could intervene in a local strike over the head of Mayor Wagner.

"What if we provide a climate for the governor to move in?" I said.

"What do you mean?" asked Corbin.

"What if we got every newspaper in New York City to editorially demand that the governor step in to prevent this thing from blowing up into a citywide riot?"

"That would be good if you can do it."

So I called Wechsler at the *Post*. By this time Evans Clark had died, and my contact at the *Times* editorial board was A. H. (Abe) Raskin. I called Raskin. I went to the *World Telegram and Sun* and to the *Daily News*. They all had editorials. Corbin and Paley were happy, and it was time for the next step.

In a day or two, Rockefeller interrupted his campaigning in Nassau County and announced he was going to call the parties in the strike together in his office in Manhattan. Meeting there were Rocky's people, the hospitals, Van Arsdale, and Bill Taylor from 1199 (the hospitals still wouldn't sit in the same room with Davis). Davis and I waited in his office at our headquarters. While we waited, Davis told me, "make sure you ask for back pay."

He'd been thinking all this time. He'd figured out that the governor had already stuck his neck out and would eventually go along. Insisting on back pay was typical of Davis's guts, foresight, and focus on the members' needs and morale. He knew back pay would be icing on the cake for them.

Paley called and told me they had a settlement.

"What about back pay?" I asked.

"You son of a bitch! What back pay?"

"They can't go back to work without back pay."

I knew Paley used to work for unions, and even though back pay is highly unusual after strikes, I added: "Come on, Hank. You're a union man."

He slammed down the phone. Davis wouldn't budge. We waited.

After a while Van Arsdale left the meeting at the governor's office and came over to our headquarters. The first thing he did was call the judge who had jurisdiction over Davis's case and get an agreement that if the strike was settled the judge would not move on the six-month sentence. Then Dave said, "Harry, what about the back pay?"

Van Arsdale didn't say a thing. He walked to the door and opened it. Then he turned around, gave us a big wink, and left.

Davis and I waited some more. *Post* columnist Murray Kempton came by and waited with us.

After what felt like a very long time, Van Arsdale called from the governor's office and said, "Okay, you got it." What we'd won was the workers' return to their jobs with back pay and the governor's public pledge to seek collective bargaining rights for all hospital workers in New York State.

The strike ended July 18, 1962, but the legislature still had to act on Rockefeller's proposal to pass the law. The fight over this was bitter. I arrived at the 1963 legislative session with high hopes. After all, we had the governor's support. But there were powerful enemies.

Among them was Raymond Corbett, president of the state AFL-CIO. Rockefeller had insisted that our bill include compulsory arbitration of contract disputes. Corbett thought this was a dangerous precedent. Although Van Arsdale supported the bill, Corbett worked against it. Most upstate legislators, who were conservative on labor issues, opposed the bill. So did the Catholic Church, which operates many hospitals. The only legislative strength we had was in New York City. To make matters worse, Davis had a heart attack and we held off discussing serious union matters with him for six months. On occasion we got messages to him that were carefully worded so as not to upset him.

We launched another campaign. Dr. King called Rockefeller and asked him to live up to his promise and force the bill through. Our media friends were with us, but in the middle of everything the newspapers in New York City were shut down by a lengthy strike. The *Times* had a West Coast edition that continued to publish, and I would get editorials into that. Wechsler had newspaper friends upstate, and with his help we got favorable editorials in places like Binghamton, Watertown, and Saranac Lake. We got 125 favorable editorials during that campaign. Paley was in charge of the assembly's printing office. We'd meet every night around eleven, and I'd give him that day's editorials. He'd get them printed up, and the next morning they'd be in the box of every single legislator.

But Rockefeller didn't have the votes. In March 1963 the legislature passed a compromise that extended collective bargaining rights to workers in voluntary health care institutions in cities with populations of one million or more. That's how you write a bill for New York City. We'd won half a loaf: We'd removed the exemption of voluntary (private, nonprofit) hospitals and nursing homes from state labor law, but only in the city. We knew we'd have to go back eventually and get the law changed statewide, but we were happy for the moment.

I called Dave, who was back in circulation by then, from Albany and told him about it. He said, "Come home by plane, and we'll have a party at my house." I usually drove or took the train to and from Albany, but I got on one of those small planes that carries about twenty people. I was exhausted and had never been on a little aircraft before. On the way home I turned green and threw up all over the plane.

The final chapter in the campaign to get collective bargaining rights throughout the state took place in 1965 when we signed up the majority of the service workers at Lawrence Hospital in the wealthy Westchester County suburb of Bronxville. We asked for an election, and the hospital said "No." So again, we went on strike.

This strike lasted fifty-five days. Bronxville is close to the Bronx city line. We'd bring busloads of members up there for big demonstrations. Wealthy, Republican Bronxville was lily-white. Most of the strikers were African Americans who lived elsewhere. The NAACP backed us, and Ossie and Ruby, who lived nearby, were often on our picket lines. We got statements from Dr. King and lots of favorable newspaper editorials. Their theme was why should a worker at Montefiore in the Bronx have the right to an election and a worker at Lawrence Hospital, ten minutes away, not have that right? Shouldn't there be statewide collective bargaining coverage for hospital workers?

We brought things to a climax at a huge Sunday demonstration outside the hospital. Henry Nicholas and John Black were our organizers there. Johnny had been hit on the head by cops so many times it was a wonder that he remained so clear-headed. He was fearless. He proposed a sit-in at one of the hospital doors. The police were there. I alerted the *Times* reporter to have his photographer ready. The cops moved in with their nightsticks, and the next day's *Times* had a front-page photo of them clubbing strikers.

That tipped the balance. There was a big call to settle the strike before things got out of control. We got another promise from Albany and ended the strike. This time the legislature promptly passed a bill extending collective bargaining statewide. Rockefeller, whom we had endorsed for governor in 1962, quickly signed it.

Unfortunately, we never got a contract at Lawrence. We returned to the hospital thirty-six years later, but lost a close election there March 29, 2001. Bronxville again became the scene of 1199 demonstrations, as members accused the hospital of using illegal threats and intimidation in its anti-union election campaign. The National Labor Relations Board (NLRB) upheld this charge in August 2001 and ordered a new election. Marching with the Bronxville pickets again in 2001 was Ossie Davis. To pass on the tradition, he brought his grandson.

There was another human interest footnote to Bronxville. We had set up a citizens' strike committee in the town, and two couples were particularly active in it. One was John Richardson, Jr., and his wife Bonnie. John was a successful lawyer and president of Radio Free Europe. The other was Harold and Virginia Turner. Harold was a member of the faculty at Columbia University. The Richardsons and the Turners were devoutly religious wealthy white Protestants who were very much affected by the civil rights movement and Dr. King.

They marched on our picket line every weekend. They put up their own money for citizens committee ads in the Bronxville paper. Their children were harassed in school, threats were made, and rocks were thrown through their windows, but they wouldn't budge in their support of the strike.

Henry Nicholas told me about them and we became close friends. I got them interviewed by Jimmy Wechsler for the *Post*. I was even able to convince Bonnie Richardson to stop wearing her mink coat on the picket line. Getting to know these two couples taught me that people very different from the types I was used to can be just as selfless and principled. It made me better able to understand and work with people with backgrounds quite different from my own.

Twenty years after the strike, I was telling the historian Gerda Lerner about Bronxville and mentioned the Richardsons.

"That's very funny," she said.

"What's so funny?" I asked.

"I spoke recently at a reception at the home of some people

named Richardson. He's now the head of the National Endowment for Democracy. When most of the guests had left they took me to their basement and showed me something they said came from the most important thing they'd ever done in their lives."

What the Richardsons showed my friend was a plaque I'd sent them after the strike. The plaque had a personal message on it I'd got from Dr. King honoring them for the stand they took.

After we got the law for statewide collective bargaining rights in 1963, our hospital membership jumped quickly to twenty thousand. Members at places we'd organized would form committees to organize nearby hospitals. We were winning elections everywhere by landslides.

By 1965 we expanded beyond service and maintenance workers and started organizing the higher-paid workers. Hospitals are very status-conscious, so we decided we wouldn't have any success unless we organized the higher-paid workers into a separate division of the union. We called it the Guild of Technical, Professional, Office and Clerical Employees. Jesse Olson, the former pharmacist, headed it. The first big Guild unit we got was when a nine hundred–member independent union at Einstein College of Medicine in the Bronx affiliated with us in 1967.

Hospital elections are held in bargaining units created by the NLRB. In the 1960s, bargaining units were divided along these lines: service and maintenance, technical, professional, and registered nurses. You have to have a separate election to unionize any one of those groups. The NLRB changes the bargaining units from time to time, and their makeup can affect the union's ability to organize, but the idea remains the same: Workers with a common interest are supposed to vote together.

We followed that pattern in our internal structure to some extent. Having a Guild Division with separate chapter meetings and separate delegate assemblies gave the more educated members a forum to discuss their professional issues such as education, lobbying, and licensing. When we started organizing registered nurses in the 1970s, we created a separate division for them also. Some people thought separation into divisions weakened the union and encouraged elitism. Others supported divisions, saying that these divisions aided organizing by offering workers smaller and more homogenous units within a large and diverse union. Our structure has been revised in recent years to reflect the union's rapid growth (through divisions based on geography) and the restructuring of the health care industry (through divisions based on hospital networks that cut across geographic lines).

We were really militant in the 1960s. Davis regarded the contract not as a set of rules but as a battleground. We had fought to survive, and we were fighting to make an accepted place for ourselves in the industry. So we operated differently from most established unions. As time passed we toned it down for various reasons: With some managements you can develop a relationship of mutual respect. Or you don't want to alienate certain members who don't like fighting the boss every day. Or you don't want the reputation of always going off half-cocked. Basically, when you get real power you don't need to flex your muscles all the time. But you have to be ready to fight if you must.

As we organized and grew through the 1960s, we became a louder voice on national issues. On any important social issue, such as civil rights, disarmament, and the Vietnam War, we were there, usually up front with our signs and our blue and white paper hats. Someone once called those 1199 hats the most valuable piece of union literature ever issued.

We remained close to Dr. King and regularly sent delegations south for marches and demonstrations. Davis walked with James Meredith in Mississippi. Other 1199ers marched in Selma. We supported the legal defense of Angela Davis. When Dr. King was assassinated in April 1968, there were memorial programs in every hospital. Coretta King became honorary chairperson of our national organizing drive when we started it the following year.

We were the first union to actively protest the war in Vietnam. In 1965, we inserted in the *Times* the first paid ad by a union on the subject. It's an appeal from 1,268 drug and hospital workers to stop the bombing and seek an immediate cease-fire. The names of the members are there in two-point type; they each paid a dollar to finance the ad. We had daylong teach-ins and sent busloads of members to antiwar demonstrations in Washington.

But we realized doing it ourselves wasn't enough. In the public's mind, labor, led by the prowar president of the AFL-CIO, George Meany, was a bunch of militaristic hard-hats. The polls showed that union members weren't any more prowar than the general public, but most labor leaders were. We felt we had to do something to show another face of labor.

In 1965 Davis agreed that I should devote most of my time to doing this. First, people like Dave Livingston of District 65, my brother Henry of the Furriers, and others created a labor division of the antiwar group SANE. Out of that grew a group we called the Labor Leadership Assembly for Peace. The leaders were Frank Rosenblum of the Amalgamated Clothing Workers, United Auto Workers (UAW) Sec. Treas. Emil Mazey, Al Hartung of the Woodworkers, and Victor Reuther of the UAW. I was the national coordinator. We had a series of conferences in Chicago and around the country. Some were attended by five hundred union leaders. Speakers included Dr. King, economist John Kenneth Galbraith, Senators Eugene McCarthy of Minnesota and Vance Hartke of Indiana—people like that.

My main pitch at the time was to talk to union leaders about the alienation of their children, who were often college students deeply opposed to the war. Years later I was at a conference in Michigan, and I met Leonard Woodcock, president of the UAW, for the first time. He came up and thanked me.

"For what?" I asked.

"In a way, for keeping my family together."

He was talking about how the Labor Leadership Assembly for Peace gave him a forum to connect with his kids by expressing his opposition to the war.

It's hard to say in retrospect if we had any real effect, but we couldn't just sit around and do nothing. One sure thing that grew out of the experience, though, was that I made a lot of national contacts that were useful later when we organized around the country and when I was building Bread and Roses. Until the Vietnam campaign, most of my activities had been close to home. I'm a New Yorker. I'm local. Vietnam expanded my horizons a little.

1199 made steady contract gains through the 1960s, but 1968

was the pinnacle. Davis had become very familiar with the structure of hospital finances. Medicare and Medicaid were passed in 1965, and hospitals were reimbursed for their costs by formulas in which the state and, to a lesser extent, the city were central. About 70 percent of hospital costs are labor. Dave understood that what we negotiated would be a "pass-through" if we could get the state to approve higher reimbursements to the hospitals.

Sitting there in his office staring into space, Dave came up with the idea for a one hundred-dollar-a-week minimum wage in the lowest-paid hospital category in the 1968 contract. The minimum at that point was seventy-eight dollars a week.

We thought he was bluffing. But as the contract deadline approached, it became clear that he meant it. Mount Sinai had a capable executive director named Norman Metzger. He went to Elliott Godoff and said, "Your president is crazy. We can't give him one hundred dollars. If he gets ninety-six it's fantastic."

Elliott tried to reason with Davis.

"No. One hundred, not one penny less," said Dave.

It almost went to a strike. At the last minute, with the governor's people in the background saying "okay," the hospitals yielded. We got the hundred-dollar minimum. We got big improvements in health and other benefits. We got introduction of a management-paid Training Fund that today helps educate ten thousand members each year.

We had almost forty thousand members by 1968. In less than ten years, they had gone from thirty-two to one hundred dollars a week.

In 1967, I got Johnny Schultz to make another film. Through interviews with workers it showed what 1199's flowering meant to tens of thousands of New Yorkers and their families. When I showed it to *Times* labor reporter Peter Millones, he tried to wipe away tears before I could get the lights back on. Millones wrote an extensive feature article about the film that appeared, with photos, in the *Times* cultural section.

One of the workers interviewed in the film used a phrase I particularly liked in describing the growth of the hospital union. We used the phrase as the name of the film. It was *Like a Beautiful Child*.

5. I Am Somebody

The Charleston Strike

THE MEMBERSHIP meeting where we reported on the hundred-dollar-a-week minimum 1968 contract settlement was pandemonium. Members cheered. They sang. They wore buttons that said, "We Did It!"

Planning the meeting, we had discussed how to use our momentum to advance an idea we'd been kicking around. I suggested that we get Coretta King to send a telegram on the subject to be read at the meeting. I drafted the telegram, and she agreed to it. It said:

> The $100 minimum is a magnificent achievement. But millions of black women outside New York City work for far less. If you are prepared to go across the country to organize them and health care workers like them, I pledge that I will go with you.

When we read the telegram to the members they stood and cheered. They were with us.

That was the beginning of our national organizing campaign. It was a logical outgrowth of our New York successes for several reasons. It was a job that needed to be done. We now had almost forty thousand dues-paying members and could afford to put organizers in the field. The civil rights and antiwar movements of the 1960s suggested to most Americans that change was possible, and we felt well positioned to help make that change happen for health care workers.

Also, Davis didn't like standing still. He'd been around long enough to know that do-nothing unions too often become corrupt. High-living union officials disgusted him. He was determined to spend whatever money we had on organizing so that none of it sat around in the union treasury giving officers bad ideas.

Davis also thought idle officers ended up fighting with each other. He'd rather keep his staff busy fighting an external enemy.

It didn't take long to find an ideal external enemy. One of our top organizers, Henry Nicholas, had some contacts in Charleston, South Carolina. He heard that workers at Medical College Hospital (MCH) of the University of South Carolina and the smaller Charleston County Hospital in Charleston were trying to organize. The two hospitals employed four hundred service workers, all of them black and all but a dozen women. William McCord, the president of MCH, had fired twelve pro-union workers on trumped-up charges. McCord was born and raised in South Africa. *Business Week* reported in its April 6, 1969 issue that when questioned about union recognition, McCord said he was "not about to turn a $25 million complex over to a bunch of people who don't have a grammar school education."

His idea of making nice to his angry black workers—many of whom were the grandchildren of slaves—was to give them Robert E. Lee's birthday as an extra holiday.

We sent Hospital Division organizer Doris Turner down to check things out. She was supposed to address an 8 P.M. meeting of hospital workers. Her plane was delayed, and she didn't get to Charleston until midnight. She rushed to the meeting place, sure everything would be all over. But she opened the door and found the place packed. They were just sitting and waiting. When Turner spoke, they hung on her every word.

We hadn't intended to start our national organizing campaign in the South, and certainly not in Charleston, a seaport that had pretty much been bypassed by the civil rights movement. The beautiful old mansions on Charleston's battery were shored up by a system of white supremacy that hadn't changed much since the Civil War. There were hundreds of places where organizing would have been easier. But here were these highly motivated workers, and they needed help.

We sent Nicholas down there (everybody called him Nick) to work full-time and report to Elliott Godoff. The immediate issue was the twelve fired workers. We decided that it was either strike while the iron was hot or forget the whole thing. We discussed it at length, and decided we couldn't walk away. The service workers at MCH struck March 20, 1969, and the service workers at County Hospital followed them out March 28.

Although the service workers were solid, there was no question of shutting down the hospitals. Management closed a few beds and continued to function. The nurses and other white technical and professional employees continued to work throughout the strike. We knew we had to make this a bigger issue. I had a long meeting with Nick, and then I called Stanley Levison, who had remained a key advisor to the Southern Christian Leadership Conference (SCLC) after Dr. King's murder the previous year.

"We're going to bomb there the way we're going," I told him. "We've got to get the SCLC to bring its whole staff in and make this a big thing."

We talked some more and decided to try to get the Reverend Ralph Abernathy, head of the SCLC, to speak at some big rallies, to get the Reverend Andrew (Andy) Young, a young tactical genius, to be in day-to-day charge of the SCLC part, and to have me build up some visibility in the press.

The SCLC was at a low point then. They had been losing momentum in the South even before Dr. King's assassination on April 4, 1968. They'd never done anything in Charleston, and they weren't used to working with unions. But they came. Abernathy announced that the SCLC was closing its office in Atlanta and that Charleston would be its headquarters until the strike was settled.

Andy Young was in overall charge. His assistant was Stoney Cooks. The Reverend James Orange worked with the young people, who followed him as if he were the Pied Piper. David White from 1199 in New York worked with Reverend Orange. Nick was in charge of the strike end—keeping up the picket lines, seeing that people were fed, and so on. Soon Godoff and I were there full-time.

Since we were white, we stayed in the background. But Andy and I would meet every morning to discuss the day's work, and we'd check back with each other every evening to see what had happened.

Things picked up. Meetings were held every night in a different church. There would be prayer meetings, vigils, and rallies. Abernathy would speak. Mary Moultrie, a striker who was a powerful orator, would speak. Nick would speak.

After the rallies, everyone would go out and march. They'd march all over town. Often they'd march to a tourist attraction, the Old Slave Mart Museum, just to make their point. They'd march to and from the big churches. The young people were well organized, sometimes boycotting school. They'd have their own marches. Sometimes they'd all dribble basketballs. When they weren't marching, the churches organized classes in black history for them.

Centered in its churches, the black community became a highly organized force in support of the strike. Strikers received free meals at restaurants, free haircuts, donations from church collections. Some even got help with house and car payments.

Community solidarity held up when the hospitals got the courts to issue injunctions against picketing and marching. A dawn-to-dusk curfew was imposed. People kept marching. The whole black population seemed to be involved. By the end of the strike, there were more than one thousand arrests. The jails were overflowing, and dozens of strikers were detained outdoors in open fields.

Abernathy spent weeks in jail, which became a problem for us because, although everyone respected his willingness to put his body on the line, when he was in jail he couldn't be out there mobilizing support. He was a terrific speaker with a sense of humor. I remember him describing the food for prisoners at Charleston County Jail.

"Every day they gave us macaroni and cheese," he'd shout. He'd pause, and then add, *"without* the cheese."

Davis came down, got arrested, and spent ten days in jail with Abernathy.

One of the arrested strikers kept a diary in jail. "I feel that I am strong tonight because the black people are marching for the first time," she wrote. "The black people are getting themselves together."

But that took some doing. At first, the city's black leaders felt they were being pushed aside by SCLC people from outside. They also worried about where all the upheaval would lead. Those problems proved to be manageable, especially with such a skilled negotiator as Andy Young in charge.

There were also frictions within the SCLC. At one meeting, SCLC organizer Carl Farris made an impassioned speech about how 1199 was running things and demeaning the SCLC. Andy replied:

"Carl, you don't know what you're talking about. If ever we had a chance to come back as an organization we've got it now, thanks to 1199. You're attacking them when you should be thanking them."

All of a sudden, the two of them were grappling, and then they were fighting on the floor. After it was over and the meeting ended, I said to Andy, "I thought you were a big believer in nonviolence."

He looked at me and smiled.

"Sometimes," he said.

The differences between Young and Farris were soon smoothed over, and by the end of the strike Farris had become a believer in organizing black and white workers.

The real problem, of course, was the response of the South Carolina authorities. They began to look on the strike as a serious threat with big stakes. They realized that if they allowed us to win, workers throughout the South would see it as an open door for organizing. They didn't want that, and they had some pretty powerful ammunition.

For one thing, both hospitals were public institutions, and South Carolina public employees were forbidden by law to unionize. South Carolina was not New York. We knew we weren't going to get that law changed. That meant we weren't going to end up with a contract. We just hoped we could get some kind of halfway victory as we had done in New York ten years earlier.

Medical College Hospital hired Knox Haynesworth to represent them. Haynesworth was the well-connected attorney for J. P. Stevens, the state's big anti-union textile firm. The hospitals got Gov. Robert McNair involved. McNair, a Democrat, called out the National Guard. They arrived in Charleston equipped with bayonets, gas masks, and tanks. It looked like a war zone. The hospitals also alerted right-wing racists Sen. Strom Thurmond and Rep. L. Mendel Rivers, both powerful South Carolina Republicans who worked against us behind the scenes. There were lots of telephoned bomb threats. Nicholas's hotel room was firebombed. Fortunately, he wasn't there.

Once again, it became clear that we weren't going to win this fight on the picket lines and streets of Charleston alone. The story was big news in Charleston and once in a while I got something in the New York papers, but my goal was to make the strike a national story.

My first breakthrough was with Murray Seegar of the *Los Angeles Times*. I got him to come to Charleston. He loved the story about Dr. McCord and Robert E. Lee's birthday, and he did a wonderful feature. The article was accompanied by cartoons that the hospital had handed out during the early days of the union campaign. The cartoons showed ugly racist depictions of primitive-looking hospital workers.

Then somebody suggested I talk to Jack Bass. Jack was the North Carolina statehouse reporter for the *Charlotte Observer*, and he was widely regarded as very knowledgeable about the South. He was also a stringer for the *New York Times*.

I got to know Jack through a series of long telephone conversations in which he tried to educate me.

"Moe, have you ever been in the South before?" he asked in one of our talks.

"No."

"Well look, before you go any further, you better get hold of the book by W. J. Cash, *The Mind of the South*, and read it so you'll understand a little bit of what you're into here."

I didn't have time to read the book, but Jack warned me of deeply ingrained racism, violence, and hostility to outside interference that he said characterized much of the South. I took his word for it. Through his advice, research on our behalf, and weekly articles in the *Times*, Jack became an important ally. Eventually, the *Times* sent its Southern reporter, Jim Wooten, to Charleston, and he did a number of stories. So did the *Washington Post*, the *Atlanta Consti-*

tution, Newsweek, and *Time.* Some of the stories were accompanied by favorable editorials. I also was able to interest Av Westin, the CBS-TV Nightly News editor, and Van Kardish of ABC-TV. I'd stress to all these people that Charleston was the most important civil rights event since Dr. King's death. I'd say that it was a reawakening of the spirit, a new possibility of changing things in the South by creating a union of black women workers, that the story had people in jail, escalating tensions, and the possibility of explosion.

We also ran a full-page ad in the *Times.* It had a top-to-bottom picture of Mrs. King's face. The copy at the top said, "If My Husband Were Alive Today," and at the bottom it continued "He Would Be in Charleston, South Carolina." The talented graphic artist Stan Glaubach designed the ad, and it was very powerful. It included an appeal for funds. We made back the cost of the ad, plus getting all that visibility. We got a lot of financial support. School kids collected money for us. 1199ers in New York made regular donations. We got a check for two hundred dollars from Jackie Kennedy. I kept a photocopy of it. A few weeks into the strike, the SCLC asked Coretta King to come to Charleston. I met her at the airport. As she walked off the tarmac, one of the reporters said, "Mrs. King, welcome to Charleston, South Vietnam." That's how tough things were, with the National Guard and the tanks and gas masks.

The enthusiasm around Mrs. King was fantastic. The national networks and reporters from all over the United States were there. She was scheduled to speak at the Morris Brown Church that night, but the crowds were so big she also had to speak at Ebenezer Baptist Church. I helped prepare her speech, and it went something like this:

Why am I here? I'm here because this is a strike by black women, black women hospital workers. One thing that hospital workers, black, white, or brown, have in common all over the country is that they are poor, they are terribly exploited, and they need a union more than anybody else. That's why I'm with you. And you can count on me to stay with you in your fight for justice, for human rights, and for dignity.

We were calling the union in Charleston 1199B by this time, so in one of her speeches we added this idea:

When we win in Charleston, it's not going to stop here. We're going to use up the whole alphabet. There will be 1199s all over the country—1199C, 1199D, 1199E, and all the way up.

That was the first mention of that idea, but it later became a reality.

Mrs. King came several times to Charleston, staying two or three days, speaking, leading prayer vigils, and marching in parades. Sometimes we'd suggest that she just sit in the strike headquarters and spend an afternoon chatting with strikers and their children. Those were very warm affairs and she loved them.

When she was out of town, she insisted that I stay in contact. She's a night person, and one night I got a call from her at two in the morning.

"I was sitting next to Senator Hubert Humphrey at a dinner tonight," she complained. "When he asked me what's new in Charleston I didn't have anything to say. You've got to keep me up to date."

So I felt comfortable calling her often. One day I asked her if we could say she'd be willing to go to jail if the strike continued much longer. She said she would, and she'd seriously consider taking her four kids with her. She added that she'd even ask Ethel Kennedy and her children to join her. While some of the strikers had actually been arrested with their children, that fortunately did not become necessary for the King or Kennedy families.

A highlight of the strike was the Mother's Day March on May 11, 1969. Ten thousand people marched. Top labor leaders from around the country came, and some said there wasn't an able-bodied black citizen of Charleston who didn't participate. There were people marching on crutches. There were nurses and nuns. Jesse Jackson, who had SCLC duties elsewhere during most of the Charleston battle, came and marched with a band. It was beautiful.

This was during the period when the UAW and the Teamsters had withdrawn from the AFL-CIO to form a separate Alliance for Labor Action. United Auto Workers Pres. Walter Reuther cut short a vacation in Denmark to be at the Mother's Day March. George Meany, president of the AFL-CIO, didn't come, but sent one of his top lieutenants, Bill Kircher. Reuther announced he had with him a twenty-five thousand dollar donation to the strikers. Kircher quickly matched this contribution.

"If the labor movement splits any more we'll make a profit," I told Andy Young.

He and I were walking at the end of the march. I asked Andy, "What do you think? Can we win this thing?"

"I don't know if we'll win, but we sure can't lose," he said.

Now that our story was being told around the country, I had to get some political people involved. William Vanden Heuvel was one. Bill was a New York lawyer who had been close to John F. Kennedy and was now an advisor to Sen. Ted Kennedy. I met him in New York through Stanley Levison, and I told him the whole story. He said Senator Kennedy was interested, and I should stay in close contact. Bill's wife, Jean Stein, who seemed to know everybody, was calling people like Joan Kennedy, columnist Tom Wicker, novelist William Styron, and feminist leader Gloria Steinem and getting them involved.

With the help of civil rights leader and current Georgia Congressman John Lewis, I got a lot of information about the strike to Ethel Kennedy, Washington lawyer Peter Edelman, and other people at the John F. Kennedy Memorial. Edelman and Vanden Heuvel were talking to Walter Mondale and people in the Senate. The story was getting around.

Communication was complicated on our end by the fact that Godoff and I knew the phones in our hotel rooms were tapped by the state, so we used pay phones on the street for anything we didn't want the authorities to know. I was always out on the sidewalk shouting over traffic noises.

One day I was talking with Jim Farmer, undersecretary of the Department of Health, Education, and Welfare (HEW). I was at a pay phone in a bar, next to a loud jukebox. I couldn't hear Farmer very well, but something I thought he said stuck in my mind. Farmer sounded uneasy when he said it, and I thought it might be important. It was about somebody having a month after May 15 to reply.

I asked Vanden Heuvel about it, and he said he'd check into it. He contacted Ruby Martin, who had been the head of HEW's Office of Civil Rights under President Lyndon Johnson. (Richard Nixon was elected to succeed Johnson in 1968, the previous year.)

Vanden Heuvel called me back and said, "I think we've fallen into something."

"What?"

"Ruby tells me that Farmer is probably referring to the fact that Medical College Hospital is in hot water with HEW over civil rights violations."

The violations, it turned out, were for things like separate drinking fountains in the hospital—the fountains for blacks were of course inferior—and other civil rights violations. The Department of Health, Education, and Welfare was investigating and fifteen million in federal building funds for the hospital were at stake. At the moment, nothing had happened. The probe had been initiated by the Democratic Johnson administration, and Nixon's Republican administration was handling the matter with kid gloves.

I thought this might be the key to everything, a way to force the hospitals to settle. Ruby Martin helped me get to the HEW people in Atlanta. I bluffed my way through with one of their head people, pretending I knew everything. They were worried.

By this time Peter Edelman had got the HEW documents on the MCH case from Martin. "They're dynamite," he told me. "I'll mail them to you in Charleston right away." I waited a couple of weeks and nothing happened. When I called Edelman, he checked with his secretary and then made a big apology.

"They sent it to you in Charleston, West Virginia, and it came back. I'll send it right away by messenger."

Mishaps like that underlined to us how we were operating on a shoestring with no support staff in a fight against sophisticated and well-heeled opponents. It was frustrating, but we were used to it and didn't have any choice.

Armed with the documents, Godoff and I set up a meeting with the Atlanta HEW people. They didn't want to be seen with us in Charleston, so they set the meeting up in a restaurant forty miles out of town. A great fish place, I remember.

The HEW guy meeting with us was Dr. Horace Brim. He told us that in addition to investigating the hospital's civil rights violations, HEW was also investigating the twelve firings. Apparently, HEW had evidence that the hospital falsely accused the twelve workers of leaving patients to attend a union meeting. If this were true, the hospital, which received federal funds, would have run afoul of HEW regulations by falsifying documents about how those funds were used.

Dr. Brim seemed eager to see the strike ended. We made clear that rehiring the twelve fired workers would have to be part of a settlement. He said they'd work on it.

Jim Wooten of the *Times* was on vacation, so, on the advice of my old friend Jimmy Wechsler at the *New York Post* (I was always calling Jimmy and asking, "What do I do now?"), I called Bruce Galphin, the *Washington Post*'s man in Atlanta. All the Washington insiders read the *Post* religiously. When I told Galphin I had an exclusive for him based on new HEW documents, he said he'd be in Charleston right away.

Galphin arrived, read the documents, and got very excited. He wrote a forty-five–paragraph feature and assured me it would be in that Sunday's *Post*. I went to New York for the weekend. On Sunday morning I got up early and drove to the Hotel Commodore in mid-Manhattan, where they carried the *Post*. I thumbed through the whole issue and nothing. Not a word. It was still early Sunday morning, but I called Jean Stein. I apologized for waking her and explained the problem.

An hour later, she called back and said she'd reached *Post* editor Ben Bradlee at his tennis club. Bradlee told her that a big breaking story had pushed Charleston off the Sunday front page, but that it would be on the Monday front page with an editorial. It was, and it had an impact. People were seeing that maybe we had the leverage we needed to reach a settlement.

Along with the publicity, we had an economic campaign going. Black people in Charleston saw the strike as a civil rights struggle against the city's white power structure. They had broadened the battlefield and were boycotting stores on King Street, the main shopping street. Their program was justice for hospital workers, but they also used the slogan "Don't Buy Where You Can't Eat." NBC-TV said the boycott cost downtown merchants fifteen million dollars.

Andy Young would hold up a dollar bill at rallies and say, "You hold onto that dollar bill and squeeze it till the eagle grins."

Bill Vanden Heuvel met with Governor McNair and local bankers to say, on behalf of Ted Kennedy, that the strike was an economic and political disaster and should be settled.

John Jay Iselin, a member of a wealthy Charleston family and president of New York public television Channel 13 (and later president of Cooper Union), met with Charleston bankers to urge a settlement. We didn't find this out until after the settlement.

Things were looking good. The HEW people in Atlanta said their Washington office would be sending the hospital a letter making rehiring the twelve fired workers a condition for continued funding of the hospital's multimillion-dollar HEW grant. We interpreted this as the basis for ending the strike.

We were ready to celebrate. Our local attorney took Godoff, Nick, Stoney Cooks, and me on a tour of the city. We never really had the time to see it before. He took us to a terrific local restaurant. We had a wonderful evening.

When we got back to the hotel, there was a message under the door from Bill Saunders, a local black militant who was in on the hospital campaign from the start.

"The settlement is off," the message said.

Pressure had come from the very top. Leon Panetta, HEW civil rights head at the time, then a Republican but later a Democrat, described what happened in a book he wrote about his break with the Nixon administration. While we were celebrating, Panetta and others were discussing the HEW Charleston crackdown in the White House office of Nixon chief of staff John Ehrlichman.

"The blacks are not where our votes are," Ehrlichman said, according to Panetta. Ehrlichman opposed putting HEW pressure on the hospital. The word filtered down, and Senator Thurmond, Representative Rivers, and the head of the South Carolina Republican Party put the heat on HEW Secretary Robert Finch. They threatened mayhem if the twelve fired workers were taken back. HEW reversed itself. The settlement was dead.

It was the worst night I had in Charleston. Andy Young was in my room.

"Okay," he said. "I guess we'll have to pick ourselves up and start all over again."

The night marches began. The SCLC's Hosea Williams led them in violation of the curfew. Hundreds of people, lots of confrontations. You could hear the sirens every night. Ralph Abernathy went to jail again and began a hunger strike.

It was getting ugly. We didn't know what to do or where we were going. There were rumors that some of the younger black militants were going to try to take over and that the city was going to erupt in violence.

Early in the strike I'd talked to top Nixon advisor Daniel Patrick Moynihan, who later became a Democratic U.S. Senator from New York. He asked me to call him whenever there was something he should know. I called him now and said, "This city is going to go, and if you don't do something you'll have it on your hands."

The next morning he called back. He said Secretary of Labor George Schultz was coming down to meet with us. We met with Schultz and a bunch of his people. They nosed around town a while and came back.

"We're going to reinstate the settlement," Schultz said.

Early in the strike, the editor of the *American Journal of Nursing*, Barbara Schutt, had put me in touch with the head of the Charleston County Nurses Association. I'd call her almost every day, and she'd tell me what was going on inside the hospitals.

As the strike settlement neared, she warned me of serious reports that the MCH nurses, all of whom were white, would refuse to work with the twelve reinstated workers. Apparently the strike had heightened racial hostility among many white workers.

I told Andy Young. We agreed that we couldn't allow this to derail the settlement. He spoke to the head of MCH, Dr. McCord, and arranged to slip in the back door of the hospital and meet with the nurses. A few hours later I called my friend from the Nurses Association and asked, "How did Andy Young do?"

"Do you have any more people like him?" she asked.

"Why?"

"At the end of the meeting they were all singing 'We Shall Overcome.' "

I saw Andy at the settlement meeting. "How did it go with the nurses?" I asked.

"All right," he said.

"How did they sing?"

"Who told you?" he asked.

The strike at MCH was settled on June 27, 1969. County Hospital settled on the same terms ten days later. The settlement did not recognize the union. It returned the twelve fired workers to their jobs and provided a grievance procedure, a credit union for handling voluntary union dues, and a wage increase that was part of a raise for all state employees. The workers at both hospitals voted enthusiastically to ratify the agreement.

Abernathy was in jail on a hunger strike when MCH settled. Nick, Godoff, our lawyer Gene Eisner, and I, and the SCLC's Carl Farris, Stoney Cooks, and Hosea Williams met with him there to discuss whether he should stay in jail until County settled. The MCH settlement included dropping all charges, so Abernathy could have walked out whenever he liked.

It was about 130 degrees in there. Abernathy's hunger-strike diet was milk occasionally spiked with smuggled-in gin. He had us kneel in prayer for what felt like forever. Finally Abernathy asked each of us whether he should stay in. I told him I agreed with everyone that in personal terms we wanted him free immediately, but in terms of PR it would be better if he stayed in jail. He did, and a couple of days later County settled.

So that was the end of what certainly had been more than a strike. In some ways it was the awakening of Charleston's black community. Changes had been set in motion that couldn't be reversed. We made a movie about the strike called *I Am Somebody*, a phrase intended to sum up the sense of self-respect the strikers gained through sacrifice, courage, and unity.

The Charleston story and the movie about it were a major help in organizing elsewhere. But hopes that the strike would lead to a real hospital union in Charleston were disappointed. We didn't have the resources to keep organizers down there. Maybe we could have if we were a bigger union, but unfortunately the structure created by the strike gradually disintegrated. Today, hospital workers in Charleston are still unorganized.

The legacy of Charleston, though, is immense. As soon as the strike ended, we sent 1199 organizers from New York to major cities around the East. The urban riots following Dr. King's death were fresh in people's memory, and every hospital administrator and trustee in the country had seen the marchers in Charleston night after night on their television screens. So had millions of hospital workers.

We quickly signed up majorities at five Baltimore hospitals, including the prestigious Johns Hopkins. Mrs. King and Baltimore Bullets basketball star Ray Scott stood in front of Hopkins shaking hands with the workers and urging them to vote union. Management agreed immediately to an election. Their idea was, "We don't want another Charleston here." We won big. The other Baltimore hospitals followed suit, and in a matter of months we had a seven thousand–member local there called 1199E.

Henry Nicholas went to Philadelphia and had a similar experience. Mrs. King appeared there too in front of places like Temple University Hospital. Before long there were ten thousand members in that city's 1199C. We had other organizing successes that grew directly out of Charleston: 1199P in Pennsylvania outside Philadelphia, 1199J in New Jersey, 1199/New England, and elsewhere. Later districts grew rapidly in West Virginia, Kentucky, Ohio, Indiana, Wisconsin, Washington State, California, and New Mexico. At New York City's huge and prestigious Presbyterian Hospital, Vice Pres. Eddie Kay led a drive that brought several thousand members into 1199, and growth continued at other major institutions in the city and the surrounding area. Mrs. King appeared in New York organizing drives at St. Luke's Hospital and elsewhere.

In 1973, 1199 in New York organized the founding convention of the National Union of Hospital and Health Care Employees, AFL-CIO. The convention made New York's 1199 one of the dozen National Union districts it had created. While most of the National Union's members were then still in the New York local, the new structure was designed to accommodate rapid national growth. By the mid-1980s, the National Union had 150,000 members, half of them in New York.

The National Union had grown dramatically and improved the lives of tens of thousands of hospital workers and their families from coast to coast. To a large extent, this was made possible by the heroism of the workers in Charleston.

6. Bread and Roses

Working People Deserve the Best

THE 1199 Bread and Roses Cultural Project has been widely acclaimed for several decades as labor's foremost arts program, and I'm as excited about it today as when we started in 1978.

But the idea for Bread and Roses seemed shaky and far-fetched when it hatched. I remember flying down to Washington, D.C., with Leon Davis in the spring of 1978. He was going to a conference—I forget what the subject was. I told him I was going to meet with some people about an idea I had for a new cultural program. When I explained it, he said, "I don't think it will ever amount to anything, but go ahead and try."

That was the humble beginning of Bread and Roses. And in a way, I got into it by default. 1199 had come of age, and I was no longer consumed by daily legislative and public relations crises that threatened our very existence. I had the time and energy to think more about the cultural programming that brought me to the labor movement in the first place. And I was ready for a change.

My first two decades at 1199 had been filled with so many dramatic events—the 1959 strike, passage of collective bargaining legislation, our rapid growth in New York's hospitals, Charleston— that the 1970s almost seemed tame.

Of course, it just seemed that way. Plenty happened in the '70s.

We continued growing outside of New York. We expanded our appeal beyond the Charleston slogan "Union Power Plus Soul

Power" in order to organize in predominantly white areas in the Midwest and New England. But we also built our strength in locals like 1199C in Philadelphia, which remained overwhelmingly black. A tragic event in the early organizing in Philadelphia came in 1972, when promising young 1199C organizer Norman Rayford was killed by a security guard in the parking lot of Metropolitan Hospital, which we were trying to organize.

We had citywide strikes in New York in 1973 and 1976.

The 1973 strike was an example of how Leon Davis was willing to buck the tide. In order to curb inflation, President Nixon had created a federal board that had to approve all union contracts. We'd negotiated annual 7.5 percent raises in 1972 in a two-year contract with the League of Voluntary Hospitals. Nixon's board rejected our second-year raise, reducing it to 5.5 percent. All other U.S. unions had accepted the Nixon board, but Davis regarded it as an unacceptable intrusion into labor relations. So we took thirty thousand workers at forty-eight hospitals out for a weeklong strike. In the end we got the raise up to 6 percent, a mere 0.5 percent increase, but Davis had made his point.

I argued against the strike, but President Nixon didn't know that. That year he named me to his private "Enemies List." As disclosed later during Watergate, Nixon drew up a list of people who were thorns in his side and told the Internal Revenue Service (IRS) to harass them with audits. I was flattered to hear I'd been selected for the list, and publicly said I'd do everything within my power to justify the President's confidence in me. I never had any trouble with the IRS.

The 1976 strike ended badly. Alarmed by hospital inflation, New York's governor, Hugh Carey, had reduced state Medicaid reimbursements for hospital costs. When we asked for raises, the hospitals said they were broke. We struck for ten days at thirty-three hospitals and got agreement for the issue to go to binding arbitration. But the award by arbitrator Margery Gootnick was very disappointing.

The 1973 and 1976 strikes, however limited the immediate results, showed that we were a major power that would stand up for hospital workers. That paid off in continued organizing, especially among nurses. We established our League of Registered Nurses, a fourth division within 1199, in 1977. One of its first successes was getting a contract for the six hundred nurses at Brookdale Hospital in Brooklyn after a two-day strike.

By the end of the '70s, we were preoccupied by two major internal issues.

One was the proposed merger of our National Union with the Service Employees International Union (SEIU). We were at that time still a part of the Retail, Wholesale and Department Store Union (RWDSU), the international union that had provided a shelter from raiding to 1199 and District 65 during the McCarthy era. But the RWDSU was small and had no health care members aside from us. We made up at least half of its total membership. Davis and others in 1199 felt if we were to truly become the nation's health care union, we needed to merge with the SEIU, which then, as now, had the nation's largest concentration of unionized health care workers. Union mergers, often a necessity in an era of corporate mergers and globalization, are never easy. So that was the subject of endless speculation, discussion, and negotiation.

The other big issue was succession. Davis, 1199's leader since he helped found the union in 1932, had a serious stroke in 1979, when he was seventy-two. He recovered, but everyone was aware that the white men who built the union in its early days would have to make way before too long for a younger generation that more closely resembled the current members, most of whom were black and Hispanic women. The big questions were when would Davis and the other veteran leaders step down and who would replace them.

These preoccupations of the late 1970s didn't require my skills as much as earlier 1199 battles had, so I was looking for new things to do. We had continued and expanded our cultural programs as we grew, but we never had the money to do any of the big ideas that were in the back of my mind.

Bread and Roses began to take shape in the spring of 1978 when Jack Golodner, director of the AFL-CIO Department of Professional Employees, told me there might be grants available from the National Endowment for the Arts (NEA) for some of the projects I dreamed of. This was during the Carter administration when federal endowments like the NEA were looking for a labor project to support. I contacted the NEA and flew to Washington to meet with their people. It was on that trip that Davis said he didn't think my plans would come to anything. This time he was wrong. The NEA saw I had some experience, and I wrote an elaborate proposal that impressed them. The result was a $15,000 six-month planning grant from them followed by a $20,000 planning grant from the National Endowment for the Humanities (NEH). My proposal in Washington needed a name, and I chose Bread and Roses. The phrase comes from a slogan used in the sixty-three–day textile strike of 1912 in Lawrence, Massachusetts, in which exploited immigrant women carried a banner reading, "We Want Bread and Roses Too." That says it all. You couldn't make up anything better. It captured what I envisioned for 1199ers: economic gains to meet their material needs and cultural programs to enrich their lives.

The first step under the planning grants was to set up a task force to chart our direction. Of course, our longtime friends Ossie Davis and Ruby Dee were on it. So were many other prominent playwrights, poets, historians, photographers, filmmakers, and political thinkers. The task force broke up into committees, each with a project.

Then I went to the 1199 Executive Council, the union's governing body of elected officers. I explained what we were doing and asked for some organizers to help as advisors. One of the organizers suggested a rank-and-file committee. I spoke at delegate assemblies and asked for volunteers. We got four hundred.

As the planning progressed, I realized we'd need more money to carry out all the ideas we were coming up with. So I started going to foundations. At first I didn't even know what a foundation was. Learning about them was slow and difficult. I just went from one person to another, making telephone calls and asking questions, and over our first half a dozen years we raised about two million dollars for Bread and Roses programming. This came from a combination of sources: the national endowments, state arts councils, progressive foundations oriented to the arts, and even a few corporate foundations. This was a big leap forward from what I had been doing before when funding was minimal and we paid performers almost nothing.

Getting grants was not all smooth sailing. Typical of the kind of snags I ran into was the day I appeared in Washington before an NEA meeting of program directors. We'd already received the planning grant but hoped to get a larger grant to actually carry out what we said we could do.

So I poured my heart out, doing my shtick. I finished, and you could hear a pin drop. Then one sarcastic guy asked, "I see you have Joe Papp's endorsement here. Is he going to do a song and dance for you?" (Joseph Papp, who created Shakespeare in the Park, was a flamboyant personality of the time.) Other people peppered me with hostile questions, and then they all filed out.

I felt awful. I stood dazed in the hallway when NEA overall program director Mary Ann Tighe found me.

"How'd it go?" she asked.

"Your people killed me," I said.

"Don't worry. We'll find ways to give you money."

She explained that I'd been talking to people whose own programs would be cut by the amount of money Bread and Roses received. We got the two-year program grant we needed.

We got off to a strong start in 1979, our first year. By we, I mean myself, program directors Morty Bauman followed by Tony Gillotte, coordinator Nonni Perry, who was a former hospital clerical worker and then an organizer, and my secretary, Louise Jonsson. We didn't want to overload ourselves with staff because we also got lots of help from the union organizers and volunteer delegates.

My frame of mind was go, go, go. We had the funding and this was my chance to show we could perform at the highest level. My wife says I'm compulsive, that when I start something I can't stop until I've done everything possible to make it as good as I can get it. Maybe that's true. But what I remember for sure is that I was determined to show the world we could give our members the best our culture has to offer. Sometimes I thought back to the phrase from

Charleston: "I am somebody!" I wanted our programs to reinforce members' feelings that their lives have value, their work is important, their hardships and joys noticed and respected.

In our attempt to do this, here are some of the programs Bread and Roses put on in 1979, our first year:

- *Harry Belafonte at Lincoln Center.* Belafonte's sold-out appearance for 1199ers at Avery Fisher Hall was his first New York concert in eighteen years.
- *Labor Day Street Fair.* Seventy-five thousand New Yorkers attended this fair on 42nd Street between Ninth and Tenth Avenues in Manhattan to enjoy food, a dozen free labor films in Theater Row auditoriums, and entertainment on two stages that included Afro-jazz, blue grass, Renaissance madrigals, ragtime, rock, and soul music. Other attractions included jugglers, comedians, dancers, stilt walkers, and the Bread and Puppet Theater Circus. 1199ers offered blood pressure tests and nutrition counseling and workers from other unions gave skill exhibits like cutting and making a fur coat, cake decoration, sewing, driving a bus, and framing a house. The latter was done by women carpenters.
- *UNICEF "Year of the Child" exhibition.* This multimedia event—with lectures, films, and live performers from Indonesia— was held in Gallery 1199, the art gallery at 1199 headquarters that remains to this day the only permanent art gallery in the country at a union headquarters. Viewers included children from 130 New York public school classes.
- *Series of interviews on the legacy of Dr. King.* The showpiece of the series was an interview of Andy Young by Bill Moyers, which was shown on the PBS-TV show *Bill Moyers' Journal* with an introduction crediting us for organizing it.
- *"Rise, Gonna Rise: Portraits of Southern Textile Workers."* Another Gallery 1199 exhibit, this one made up of photos by labor photojournalist Earl Dotter. With the cooperation of the Amalgamated Clothing and Textile Workers Union, we got textile workers from North Carolina to appear regularly at the gallery as resource people for visiting students.
- *Theater 1199.* Programs at union headquarters included Ossie Davis and Ruby Dee, blues and folksinger Odetta,

folksinger Pete Seeger, and my old friend Sam Levenson, the humorist.

- *Theater in the Hospitals.* Free lunch-hour performances of calypso, soul, and gospel music by the Howard Roberts Chorale at thirty New York City hospitals and nursing homes.
- *Latin Cultural Festival.* This well-attended festival included evenings with percussionist Mongo Santamaria and his eight-piece Afro-Cuban jazz group, the Puerto Rican Traveling Theater, and singer Roy Brown.
- *Bread and Roses poster.* Designed by leading graphic artist Paul Davis, the poster was circulated widely in union halls, subway stations, and national publications. It shows the head and shoulders of a proud black woman garlanded with roses and stalks of wheat.
- *"I Just Wanted Someone to Know."* A one-act musical about working women. This Labor Theater production toured for two weeks, visiting thirty-seven New York City and Pennsylvania institutions.
- *"The Working American."* A Gallery 1199 exhibit of historical paintings of Americans at work. The exhibit included an art history symposium.
- *Conferences and lectures.* Topics included patient care, occupational hazards, women in health care, the history of hospitals, and other health care subjects.

The conference on patient care, "Patient Care: The Health Care Employee's Responsibility," discussed a subject as timely then as it is now: how to reconcile optimum patient care with union contracts safeguarding working conditions. The daylong event drew 350 members, management personnel, and patient advocates to union headquarters. They were spellbound by Thomas Clancy, a wheelchair-bound quadriplegic who had spent thirteen years in New York's Goldwater Hospital:

"The person who touches you at the right time, holds your hand, or says something insignificant but magical . . . These images are implanted in your mind forever," said Clancy.

He went on to urge health care workers to address such issues as patients' right to know, patients' privacy, understanding patients' anger, refusing to cover up for coworkers' misdeeds, getting management to listen more to workers who have direct contact with patients, eliminating the elitist attitudes some supervisors have toward less-skilled workers, reducing impersonality in crucial hospital departments like the emergency room, admissions, and pre-op, and understaffing.

This conference was followed by a series of smaller conferences at individual hospitals and nursing homes. These conferences in turn created ongoing patient care committees at each institution. The job of the committees was to act on issues discussed at the conferences.

Staffing was a major issue at nearly all our patient care gatherings. I remember a registered nurse (RN) at the Beth Israel Medical Center conference in Manhattan who was nearly in tears herself as she said that understaffing "doesn't leave you time to sit down with a patient who is crying." That nurse wasn't alone. Many 1199ers feel indignant when understaffing prevents them from giving the kind of personal care each patient deserves. Our Bread and Roses patient care program established in a public and dramatic way that 1199 members care deeply about providing the best health care possible.

A recent example of 1199ers' dedication is the tragic story of David Marc Sullins, the Cabrini Medical Center emergency medical technician who died September 11, 2001, at the World Trade Center. Sullins, the thirty-year-old father of two young sons, had just finished his shift when word came of the WTC disaster. With coworkers, he raced to the scene. Others tried to prevent him from going in, urging him to help the injured who had made it out to the street. But Sullins insisted the people inside needed him more. He went in and never came out.

The 1979 Bread and Roses events were just a warm-up. We continued along the same lines in 1980, but added several major new events.

One was Bread and Roses Day in Lawrence, Massachusetts. Our theme for the April 27 event was "A Commemoration of the City that History Forgot." As in many other American labor struggles, the epic 1912 Lawrence textile strike was too soon forgotten by the community where it took place, and I wanted to help change that.

I was always fascinated by the story of the strike and by its parallels to 1199's own struggles. Some twenty-three thousand workers, most immigrant women and children, walked out spontaneously in January 1912 when their six-dollar-a-week wages were lowered. The strike that followed became national news and was unlike any earlier American labor struggle. It was conducted by immigrant women and children who came from forty-five countries and spoke thirty-six languages. But when they sang labor songs together it was with one voice.

The strike had a heart. The workers were always marching and singing. They put on shows, dances, and debates. It was like a workers' university with a short course on the class struggle. And of course, this was the strike where workers carried the sign, "We Want Bread and Roses Too."

Despite ferocious opposition, including National Guardsmen with bayonets, as in Charleston, the strikers won major wage gains. And congressional investigations exposed the exploitation of Lawrence workers for the entire nation to see.

I knew Ralph Fasanella, a highly acclaimed self-taught artist, had spent two years up in Lawrence doing paintings about the strike. I knew because I had suggested it to him. I also remembered *Milltown*, a powerful but out-of-print photo and caption book about the strike by Bill Cahn, an old friend of mine who had died of cancer. Before he died Bill asked if I could try to get the book reissued. With the help of Paul Sherry, a leader of the United Church of Christ (UCC), we reissued the book as *Lawrence 1912: The Bread and Roses Strike*. The UCC's Pilgrim Press printed it with an introductory essay by journalist Paul Cowan, who died too young soon afterward.

From there we developed a film on the strike narrated by Ruby Dee and using the Judy Collins song "Bread and Roses." The film was later used extensively by Lawrence schools, unions, and community organizations. We had a six-week exhibition in Gallery 1199 of Fasanella's paintings, which were widely displayed in Lawrence.

Paul Cowan had been interested in Lawrence for some time. He was struck by the community's almost total amnesia about the strike. Here's an example that he uncovered:

A pivotal event had been the 1912 testimony before a congressional committee of thirteen-year-old Lawrence striker Camella Teoli. The committee hearings were attended by influential people such as the wife of then-President William Howard Taft. Camella told how she had been partially scalped when her hair caught in a cotton-twisting machine. The factory then dismissed her without compensation. Testimony by Lawrence workers like Camella led to adoption of the country's first child labor laws. Sixty-three years later, Cowan sought out Camella Teoli's daughter. He was amazed to find that while the daughter remembered combing her mother's remaining hair into a bun to cover the bald spot, she didn't know of the accident that caused the baldness.

When Cowan showed her the congressional testimony of her mother, the daughter said, "Now I have a past. Now my son has a history."

Camella Teoli's daughter was not alone. An article on the strike, which Cowan wrote for the *Village Voice,* was distributed in Lawrence in the late 1970s by the Lawrence Historical Society, and a reawakening of the community's memory had begun. The subject was being debated on talk radio, and Mayor Lawrence LeFebre, whose parents had been immigrant French Canadian mill workers, wanted the strike's history revived.

So with the help of Paul Sherry, Mayor LeFebre, Paul Cowan and his wife Rachel, and Margo Jones, a New York City elementary school teacher who later became a valuable Bread and Roses staff member, we organized a Bread and Roses Day in Lawrence for April 27, 1980.

The day was a huge success, both with the national press and the people of Lawrence. It started when the local high school band marched into our outdoor rally playing "Solidarity Forever." Students held banners saying "bread and roses" in the thirty-six languages spoken by the 1912 immigrant strikers. Mayor LeFebre renamed a street after Camella Teoli, and in a skit the local students reenacted her testimony. Mary Travers and Peter Yarrow of Peter, Paul and Mary sang labor songs. Our film was shown, and prominent political and labor leaders spoke. Then food prepared by the people of Lawrence was served indoors, and on every table was a white tablecloth with a loaf of bread and a red rose.

I met and worked with some wonderful people on Bread and Roses Day in Lawrence, and I'm lucky that our friendship continues to the present. They include Paul Sherry; Margo Jones; Rachel Cowan, who later wrote an important article on the project for the *Village Voice*; and Esther Cohen, a gifted writer and editor who was then with Pilgrim Press and has since become the highly effective creative director of Bread and Roses.

Another project in 1980 was the musical revue *Take Care*. Although I drew from my *Thursdays 'Til Nine* experience in producing *Take Care*, there were some major innovations. At the suggestion of Eve Merriam, our first creative step to gather material was a fourteen-week series of workshops in which author Lewis Cole discussed with hospital workers the details of their jobs and home lives. This was very productive.

Members told about their workday—"from the kitchen aide who helped infirm patients spoon down their food to the admitting clerk who sometimes had to chase kids off her desk"—recalled Cole. Participants were proud of their work and felt they got inadequate recognition, but at first were reluctant to say anything that would reflect badly on their institution. After a while they opened up and began to discuss issues like the disproportionately high number of low-paid workers who were female, frictions between RNs and lower-skilled personnel, on-the-job racism, overbearing doctors, and ethical issues such as whether a frequently pregnant drug addict should be sterilized.

Once the workshop material was collected, it was transformed into songs and sketches by Ossie Davis, Mikki Grant, Merriam, Alan Menken (winner of two Academy Awards), Cole, and composer Helen Miller. The writers said the show virtually wrote itself because of the material from the workshops. *Take Care* included numbers called "Burnout" ("You tell it, girl!" audiences shouted), "Young People Today," "Getting Up, Getting Out," "Woman to Woman," "Night Worker: Midnight Morning," and "Delegate Blues" sung by five professional performers accompanied by three musicians.

Take Care toured forty-five 1199 hospitals in New York. We passed around forms to members in the audience and asked them to write down what they thought of the show.

A Presbyterian Hospital nurse's aide wrote, "It's a rare treat, because normally only doctors and nurses are considered fitting subjects for television and musicals about hospital life."

A clerk–typist at Montefiore wrote, "It was like seeing a Broadway show for free."

Take Care made an eleven-state tour in which it was seen by more than thirty-five thousand hospital workers. Its finale was at the Department of Labor auditorium in Washington, where it was hosted by Secretary of Labor Ray Marshall, Jr., Federal Council of the Arts and Humanities chair Joan Mondale, and the heads of the NEA and NEH.

Among the many press reviews of *Take Care* was this, by *Wall Street Journal* labor editor Joanne Lublin:

> A sprightly new musical that realistically depicts the human dimensions of otherwise nameless stereotypes . . . clever lyrics, footstomping music and heartfelt singing . . . But you can only see it if you're a hospital worker or a patient, so if you want to catch "Take Care" at your local hospital, break a leg.

The *Village Voice* added this observation:

> "Take Care" contains not one single call to "build the union." Someone up there understood that laughing together automatically builds the union.

Soon after *Take Care* closed we began working on the "Images of Labor" poster series. The idea originated twenty years earlier in conversations I had with Stan Glaubach. We used to admire a series of ads by the Container Corporation of America in which pithy quotes were matched with works by great artists. "If only we could do something like that some day for labor," we said to each other. Stan died of a heart attack in 1973, when he was only forty-nine, but we ultimately made his dream real.

The first step was to assemble thirty-two historically significant quotes on labor from workers, poets, presidents, labor leaders, and so on. Then, with the help of curators Nina Felshin and Pamela Vassil, we asked artists to illustrate the quotes. Artists who participated included Jacob Lawrence, Alice Neel, Milton Glaser, Sue Coe, Paul Davis, May Stevens, Benny Andrews, Edward Sorel, James McMullan, Marshall Arisman, Judy Chicago, Daniel Maffia, and Ralph Fasanella.

Glaser painted a dove emerging from a pair of bound hands to illustrate the words of Nicola Sacco, the Massachusetts immigrant anarchist who was framed and executed along with Bartolomeo Vanzetti in 1927: "It is true, indeed, that they can execute the body, but they cannot execute the idea which is bound to live." Glaser's poster was reproduced by the Swedish labor movement and distributed to union halls, schools, and community groups throughout Sweden.

Sorel did a haunting drawing of crowded, hunched-over boys sorting coal outside a Pennsylvania mine. The quote from financier George Baer, commenting in 1902 on immigrant workers in his mines, was, "They don't suffer; they can't even speak English."

Davis painted a lovely pastoral scene of a swallow soaring over men hand-mowing wheat. The text came from the Old Testament: "Man was born to labor as the bird to fly."

Stevens did a portrait of black feminist Lucy Parsons to accompany Parsons' words at the founding convention in 1905 of the Industrial Workers of the World: "We are the slaves of slaves. We are exploited more ruthlessly than men."

Coe painted a black worker looming over a factory scene to illustrate the words of an anonymous worker during an Akron, Ohio, rubber factory sit-down strike in 1936. The quotation was, "We were nervous and we didn't know we could do it. Those machines had kept going as long as we could remember. When we finally pulled the switch and there was some quiet, I finally remembered something . . . that I was a human being, that I could stop those machines, that I was better than those machines anytime . . ."

Maffia's painting of two women linked by lightning illustrated the Knights of Labor motto, "An injury to one is an injury to all."

One unusual aspect of "Images of Labor" was the agreement of such prominent artists to illustrate quotes assigned to them. Under ordinary circumstances this would have seemed like an unacceptable intrusion into artistic freedom. But only one of the artists complained. We gave her a quote from George Meany, and she said she wouldn't illustrate it. We were well along in the project, and I felt I had no choice other than to tell her we'd look for another artist. She called back the next day and agreed to do it.

After a six-week exhibit in Gallery 1199 in 1981, "Images of Labor" toured U.S. museums starting at the Smithsonian Institution in Washington, D.C. It was displayed for a year in Sweden. It was seen in Italy and was the inspiration for a series of annual rock concerts called "Bread and Roses" put on by Britain's Trades Union Congress. In its four-year tour, "Images of Labor" was seen by more than half a million people. Pilgrim Press printed the posters in book form with an introductory essay by Irving Howe. It has sold eighty thousand copies to date. We've sold sixty-five thousand sets of the poster series. The posters are still being ordered through our brisk mail-order operation. People have told me of seeing "Images of Labor" posters in union offices, schools, libraries, and homes all across the country and around the world.

Unions from the American Federation of Teachers to the National Football League Players Association bought large quantities of "Images of Labor" to distribute to their members. The AFL-CIO in Washington agonized over doing the same. Finally, one of their people came to me and said, "It's great, but why do you have to have left-wing people like Woody Guthrie in it?" (One of the "Images of Labor" quotes was from folksinger Guthrie, author of "This Land Is Your Land" and many other songs that are still sung today.) In the end, the AFL-CIO leaders ordered a hundred copies to circulate among the union presidents in the AFL-CIO Executive Council. That was the kind of imagination the AFL-CIO leaders had in those days.

As a summary of the intent of "Images of Labor," I like these words, spoken in April 1981 to a New York *Daily News* reporter by novelist E. L. Doctorow:

It is the presumption of "Images of Labor" that work with the hands, the back, the concentrating eye is what most of us do in this country and few of us hear about; that from the tumultuous history of the American working people we will most surely derive our honor as a nation; and that our spiritual attention to this matter begins most properly with our artists.

These were some of the early highlights of Bread and Roses. As I mentioned, we got off with a bang in 1979 and had a lot of momentum. Then we got sidetracked for a few years by the internal dissension that plagued 1199 in the 1980s. I'll get to that in the next chapter. Bread and Roses never died, though. And it came back as strong as ever in the 1990s. While I've been executive director of Bread and Roses since it started in 1978, the program for the past several years has been booming under the day-to-day leadership of Creative Director Esther Cohen.

We've now had more than three hundred exhibits over the years in Gallery 1199. We've produced and sold all kinds of records. We've sold eighty-five thousand posters from our five widely displayed "Women of Hope" poster sets (African American, Latina, Asian American, Native American, and international). Our annual arts projects in New York City schools under the direction of Margo Jones have involved thousands of children and produced touring exhibits of students' work entitled "Working," "Sweatshops," and "Why Unions Matter." We have a monthly Café 1199 at union headquarters where members relax, have a meal, read their own poetry, and sing their own songs. At our weekly creative writing classes, members read and critique each other's work. Our 2001 calendar featuring the paintings of Ralph Fasanella sold more than sixty thousand copies. And there's much, much more.

As I write this, our innovative Unseen America program is growing by leaps and bounds. The program provides a voice to people who are often ignored in the mainstream media through weekly classes that combine photography and writing. The end result with each group is a captioned photo exhibit. We started in New York with groups such as 1199 home care workers, SEIU Local 32B-J janitors and doormen, Filipino nannies, immigrant Chinese garment and restaurant workers, domestic violence victims, migrant farm workers, immigrant construction laborers, autistic children, and the homeless. Media coverage of Unseen America brought calls from all over, and the program has spread around the country.

Another current Bread and Roses effort is "A Day in the Life of Working New York." For this project, photographers followed workers from some twenty unions during a typical day's work. The resulting images were shown at Gallery 1199 in the fall of 2001.

Since 1199 affiliated in 1998 with the SEIU, we've worked closely with the SEIU Greenhouse cultural program and see enormous potential in that alliance. We're proud that recently the AFL-CIO, in setting up a permanent educational and cultural department, used the Bread and Roses model in developing art exhibits, concerts, lectures, and other activities.

BREAD and Roses grew out of a tradition in which culture was often used as a tool in articulating and working toward the vision of a fairer, more humane world. That tradition was strong at 1199 when I got there. In that sense, as in others, I was lucky. 1199 was a growing union, its members were receptive to cultural programs, and its president admired the world of art and beauty. Leon Davis was an unusual man. He loved the theater and he went often. He was a brilliant self-made intellectual who hated academic ivory towers, and he wanted his members to have the best that New York's cultural world could offer. He believed nothing was too good for working people. He also understood that our programs increased member involvement with their union. As a result, he supported everything I wanted to do in the cultural area. 1199's current president, Dennis Rivera, has continued that tradition by giving his wholehearted backing to Bread and Roses.

So I was lucky to be in the right place at the right time at 1199. But I also brought something to the table. Because of my background and experience, going all the way back to the Foner brothers band and my early work at other unions, when I got to 1199 I was able to both generate ideas and carry them out.

Ideas are the easy part. You can put a group of smart people in a room and come up with all kinds of fantastic concepts. The hard part is making them happen. When I first went to the endowments in 1978, I'm sure they said to themselves, "We've heard this kind of stuff before, but not from a union. We'll give 1199 a shot because we need a labor program. But chances are this guy Foner will never do half of what he says he'll do."

We proved the doubters wrong. We made all of those ideas work. Part of the reason was my experience. Another was follow-through. In some unions, you could suggest a project and go around the room and all the leaders would say, "That's great. Let's do it." Then nothing would happen. That's not how it was at 1199. A big thing we had going for us at 1199 was our organizational structure and spirit. Few other unions could have done what we did because few had the closeness we had among organizers, delegates, and members.

At 1199, we could reach out to members and bring them to our programs. We could find thoughtful, articulate members who would tell us what kind of programming worked. We had experience with organizers selling tickets—and keeping track of the money responsibly—so that we'd know what kind of attendance we could expect for our events. We built lists of members who had come to our events in the past and did special advance mailings to them about upcoming events. Every show we had, we performed first for the delegate assemblies. That way we had many hundreds of delegates who could go to their members and say, "I've seen it and it's wonderful. You've got to come." These nuts-and-bolts things make the difference between success and failure, and 1199 had decades of experience with them when we started Bread and Roses.

SOME people have criticized Bread and Roses for our insistence on top-quality programs that usually involve the participation of professionals. They say we should sacrifice quality in order to get more members involved. But I don't think it's an either–or proposition. There's a place for members' work. We've had member art shows in Gallery 1199, and our popular Café 1199 and writing classes are opportunities for members to be creative.

But I've never been willing to settle for just amateur night. It's unrealistic to think that if you get a lot of workers painting, for instance, you'll get a lot of great art. What you'll get is an opportunity for a lot of people to be creative, which is very important. But we need more than that.

We need professional, trained, talented people. Our stuff has to be really good. Union members watch television. They're geared to high professional quality. They're not going to go out of their way very often for less. Maybe they'll attend once in a while when programs involve people they know, but in general they won't.

So we aim for both. We try to provide places where members can create, and we also insist on top professional quality in our programming.

A difficult question that comes up in this connection involves the racial and ethnic backgrounds of the artists we work with. We want to get the best, and we also try to get artists whose backgrounds are consistent with the subject matter. For instance, our photographer for the Native American "Women of Hope" poster series was a Native American woman. She felt strongly that the designer for the posters should also be a Native American. She had someone specific in mind. But we had a top-notch non–Native American whose qualifications we thought were better, and we chose her. While diversity usually improves quality, you can't be mechanical about it. When conflict on this issue surfaces from time to time, we've tried to treat it with balance and common sense.

Another criticism comes from people who say programs like Bread and Roses are fluff, even distractions from members' serious bread-and-butter concerns. Of course, I disagree. At 1199, which has grown from 5,000 to 210,000 New York members in the past forty years, our experience has been that cultural programs are a vital part of our work.

In the first place, as Davis said, union members do deserve the best. They deserve beauty and laughter and song and wisdom. They may get these things in their families, churches, museums, libraries, or schools. But they should get them from their union, too. When we had programs at Lincoln Center, which is expensive to rent, people would sometimes ask me, "Why does it have to be Lincoln Center?"

Because our members have never been there," I'd say.

BESIDES that, cultural activities effectively serve union interests in many ways.

They certainly help our public image. Being known as the Bread and Roses union is so powerful, so sweet and nonthreatening, that it encourages the world to see us more favorably.

This includes a positive image with unorganized workers. For instance, we'd sometimes show *Take Care* at places where we were organizing RNs. Organizers have told me our reputation helps win elections. Management must feel that way too. When our "Working American" exhibit was about to open at the University of Rochester's Memorial Art Museum, some hospital managers went to the museum and protested. We were organizing in the area, and management put the heat on the museum to cancel. But the museum stood fast, and I remember how excited I was to see one hundred of our Rochester members at the opening who had never been in a museum before in their lives.

The more important Bread and Roses benefits are long term. Our cultural activities sometimes contain social messages that advance union principles such as solidarity, opposition to racism, and support for women's rights. Members can ignore the message if they want, but it's out there to teach and motivate those who are receptive.

Just as often, though, our cultural activities aren't advancing any value system. They're just plain entertaining. That too has an important function. Those programs implicitly say, "1199 is not just another big impersonal bureaucracy like your employer or your government. Sure, we see you as a member who pays dues, and we expect you to support your fellow members in a crunch. But we also see you as a whole person who has kids, pays rent, goes to church, worries about crime and drugs, and just likes to have a good time." This silent message knits closer bonds between members and their union.

When people question the value of union cultural programs, I think back to the night in 1979 when Harry Belafonte sang to twenty-eight hundred members at Lincoln Center. In between his dazzling versions of "Day-O," "Matilda," "Kingston Town," and "Hole in the Bucket," Belafonte would stop, walk to the footlights, and tell members how happy he was to perform for their union. He'd reminisce about the many 1199 picket lines he'd been on. "On every issue worth fighting for, 1199 has been there," he told the crowd.

A nurses aide who was there that night told me she felt "it was like he was reaching over the footlights to me." How many leaflets or speeches do you think it would take to build that kind of proud identification of a worker with her union?

Besides, Bread and Roses is like chicken soup. It may not cure all your ailments, but it sure can't hurt.

I've received some gratifying recognition over the years for the achievements of Bread and Roses. *Business Week* magazine called Bread and Roses "the most important cultural program organized by a labor union." *Ms.* magazine gave me a "Hero Award" for "making the arts a living part of labor organizing." Joe Papp called me "the Joe Papp of the labor movement." The New School University awarded me an honorary doctorate in May 2000 for my "passion for bringing the arts to all Americans."

Praise can't hurt, and I'm glad we got it. But my main satisfactions come from the work itself. I remember the answer Philip Murray, president of the CIO, gave back in the 1940s when he was asked what labor wants.

"Paintings on the wall, carpets on the floor and music in the home," said Murray. I never forgot that answer, and I'm glad I've been able to help make some of it happen. My feelings were best expressed in the following Japanese haiku poem, written by Kitahara Hakushu (1885–1942) and sent to *1199 News* in 1979 by schoolteacher Amy Bookbinder of Northampton, Massachusetts:

> I have bought bread
> And I have been given
>   Red roses:
>   How happy I am
> To hold both in my hands!

7. The Busted Stradivarius

Fighting to Preserve 1199's Ideals

THE CIVIL WAR in 1199 during the early 1980s was the most heart-breaking experience of my life. For several years, it looked like all we'd worked to build would be destroyed. The issue that nearly wrecked 1199 was succession to a new generation of leaders after the retirement of Leon Davis in 1981 at the age of seventy-four.

Looking back, our problems were predictable. Labor history is full of internal battles following the departure of strong leaders. But our experience—with its bitter elements of racism, sexism, red-baiting, violence, and corruption—was worse than anyone anticipated. And it was especially difficult for those who had come to regard 1199 as a beacon of hope. The stunned reaction of David Livingston, the president of District 65, summed up the feelings of many New Yorkers.

"How do you fix a busted Stradivarius?" asked Livingston during a discussion of 1199's troubles.

Davis had made it clear for several years that he was planning to retire as president of both the National Union and of what was then called District 1199 in New York, and that he expected his successors to be African American or Hispanic.

This was as it should have been. Most of the members of District 1199 were African American, and the New York membership was approximately 20 percent Hispanic. While the figures were lower in the National Union, they were still substantial. Our goal in organizing minority workers was empowerment, and we didn't intend to stop when it came to the election of officers.

Davis had indicated publicly that he wanted District 1199 Exec. Vice Pres. Doris Turner to succeed him in New York and National Union Sec. Treas. Henry Nicholas to take over nationally. Turner and Nicholas are African Americans.

The transition to Nicholas went relatively smoothly. After Davis stepped down, the National Union convention elected Nicholas president in December 1981.

The transition to Turner following Davis's retirement and her un-opposed election as president by the District 1199 membership in April 1982 was a different story.

Doris Turner joined the 1199 staff after being a 1959 strike leader at Lenox Hill Hospital, where she was a dietary clerk. She was aggressive and outgoing, and she rose quickly to head the union's largest division, the Hospital Division.

Davis saw how closely the black women who were the majority of the Hospital Division identified with Turner, and he took her under his wing. The process of grooming her for leadership was managed badly, with terrible consequences.

It was clear that while Turner was quite effective in pursuing local problems, she had little understanding of bigger issues, both inside and outside the union. Worse, she showed no interest in learning.

Davis tried to get her to read a newspaper every day. She wouldn't. Davis asked her to spend time regularly in his office, learning what a president does. She came a few times and then stopped. With other staff members, Davis was brutal in his criticism. But he never criticized Turner. Even after others suggested to him that she might be a bad choice, he stuck with her.

Some critics called Davis patronizing and even racist. They said that by overlooking Turner's obvious flaws he was implying that nothing more could be expected from a black woman. All of us are to some extent prisoners of our upbringing, and Davis, who was born in an eastern European ghetto nearly a hundred years ago, certainly had his flaws. But being a racist was not one of them. Dave was passionate about justice, and to achieve it he was tough on himself and tough on others, whatever their race. Plenty of present and former 1199 staff members, both black and white, will testify to that.

Why wasn't he tough on Turner? I think he wanted her so much to be a success that he deluded himself about her character and capabilities. He wanted so much to crown his achievements with a successful transition to an African American woman that he blinded himself to the facts. Also, regardless of Davis's role, Turner had a personal responsibility to prepare herself for union leadership, and she failed to meet that responsibility.

The first indication that Turner might be at odds with the rest of the leadership came in our 1978 negotiations with the League of Voluntary Hospitals. Turner was especially interested in getting every other weekend off (we called it EOWO) for her members. Weekend work is hard for mothers of small children, and although most had de facto EOWO, Turner wanted it guaranteed. Davis preferred to unite the membership with contract gains that were more widely shared. He went for wages and health benefits rather than EOWO. At the meeting where members ratified the agreement, Turner sat on the stage apart from the rest of the officers, frowning. Her message was clear.

Then came the question of the merger with the SEIU. Davis had decided we'd gone as far as we could go without merging the National Union (and with it, District 1199 in New York, which was part of the National Union) with a bigger international union. The SEIU had nearly a million members, 350,000 of them health care workers in the private sector. It seemed the logical way to go.

In the AFL-CIO, mergers are done from the top down by international unions. Since we belonged to the Retail, Wholesale and Department Store Union (RWDSU), Davis went to RWDSU Pres. Al Heaps and suggested that RWDSU merge with SEIU. Heaps agreed. The members of the National Union and of District 1199 in New York voted overwhelmingly for the merger. By 1981 we were treating merger with SEIU as a sure thing.

Turner, however, was increasingly uncomfortable with the idea. Perhaps she saw herself becoming a small frog in a big pond. Whatever the reason, she had become a vocal opponent of the merger by the end of 1981. And then came the bombing.

On the day before New Year's Eve in 1981, Heaps was sitting at his desk in midtown Manhattan when a package arrived. When he tore open the wrapping, the package exploded, ripping open his stomach and nearly killing him. Heaps recovered, but one of the first things he said from his hospital bed was "the merger is off."

No one I know has ever figured out why Heaps changed his mind. No one was ever charged with the bombing, and there's no hard evidence to support the many rumors about who did it. Some thought it might have been crooked RWDSU officials who felt that while Heaps let them do what they wanted, the SEIU might not. I don't know. The whole horrible affair remains a mystery to this day, as does Heaps' about-face on the merger. I've always suspected he had major reservations about the merger from the start and used the bombing as a convenient reason to pull out.

Although the fight went on for a couple more years, without the approval of Heaps and his successor, Lenore Miller, the merger was dead. It was a lingering and messy death. The National Union continued to press the RWDSU to merge with the SEIU. The RWDSU leaders, backed by Turner, responded by trying to place the National Union in trusteeship. The ugly battle drained more and more of the National Union's resources and energies from organizing to legal defense against the trusteeship effort. Finally, in 1984, a compromise was reached. The AFL-CIO agreed to allow the National Union to withdraw from the RWDSU with an AFL-CIO charter of its own. The price was that the Turner-led 1199 in New York remained in the RWDSU.

Davis's dream had been one big union for all health care workers. But this solution resulted in three health care unions: the SEIU, the RWDSU (with 1199's seventy-five thousand New York members), and the National Union (with seventy-five thousand members in a dozen districts around the country but none in New York). Dave, watching from retirement in Florida, was shattered.

In New York, things in 1199 went from bad to worse. Turner had watched for years as Davis fully exercised the many powers given him by the 1199 bylaws. He had been a very strong president, and she intended to be one too. Whenever anyone questioned her decisions, she'd play the race card. She'd say, "If it was okay for a white man to be the boss, why not a black woman?" That was hard to deal with. It overlooked the fact that despite his intimidating manner, Davis carefully observed all the constitutional forms—which Turner did not. And Davis was a dominating president only after decades of learning by doing. Still, in our union with our membership, Turner got a lot of mileage out of labeling her opponents racists.

Over the years, without our paying attention, Turner had built a strong internal organization of staff people whose main recommendation—and sometimes only recommendation—was loyalty to her. As president, she persecuted staffers who opposed her in any way, withholding paychecks and calling people communists and sexists as well as racists. Sometimes the persecution was physical. At one Executive Board meeting, Turner attacked the union's legislative director, Judy Berek, who is now a top federal health care official. Turner scratched Berek's face, drawing blood. At another Council meeting, several Turner supporters rushed at Vice Pres. Eddie Kay and punched him as he sat at the long conference table. Kay's tires were slashed at a staff retreat. Delegate assemblies turned into chair-throwing circuses. Turner's inner circle included a number of armed staff members with prison records. Staffers Turner disapproved of received telephoned death threats. In a short time, Turner fired or forced the resignation of eighty of the union's best organizers and officers.

The merger was not the only issue on which Turner disagreed with those who were loyal to Davis. She moved the union to the right politically. At one Executive Council meeting she ignored Robert's Rules by voting from the chair to force an 8-8 tie that prevented the union from endorsing the more liberal candidate, Mario Cuomo, in his Democratic gubernatorial primary contest with Edward Koch. She opposed the anti-apartheid boycott of South Africa and refused to participate in the huge June 12, 1982, anti–nuclear weapons rally in Central Park. By contrast, I was involved in the early planning for June 12 and National Union Exec. Vice Pres. Bob Muehlenkamp was a key organizer of the event.

In the cultural area, Turner substituted religion for working-class solidarity, perhaps pleasing Protestant churchgoers but excluding the rest of the members.

Reports of financial corruption under Turner were persistent enough that a federal grand jury was impaneled to investigate. The probe was dropped later when Turner left the scene after losing her 1986 bid for reelection.

Turner never trusted me. She mistakenly thought that because of the publicity I got through Bread and Roses, I was her rival for the presidency. That was the last thing on my mind, as I repeatedly told everyone. But for years she'd been distant. She also was uncooperative on Bread and Roses projects. Then, in the 1982 contract negotiations, she told me not to speak to the press. Instead, she paid sixty thousand dollars to a public relations firm whose only function seemed to be to say, "No comment."

Being muzzled in the union where my work with the press had been so important hurt and angered me. It was the last straw. I retired as 1199's executive secretary in November 1982. Since it was my active membership in District 1199 that entitled me to be a National Union officer, in 1983 I retired as executive secretary of the National Union also. Because Bread and Roses had been set up as a separate and independent entity, I was able to remain as its executive director.

But with no base of members in New York, my ability to produce programs was limited. I worked for Bread and Roses two days a week and found a job for three days a week trying to build a cultural program at Local 342 of the Amalgamated Meat Cutters Union in Queens. Part of the program was an oral history project called "A Slice of Life." I stayed with Local 342 for three years, until March 1986. We just didn't click.

This was a low point in my life. I was a healthy and vigorous 67. I felt I still had a lot to achieve, and I wasn't prepared to fold my tent and slip away. Anne had a distinguished career at Rutgers where she was not only teaching, working with graduate students and chairing the department, but also involved in professional conferences throughout the country and writing articles and books on sociological analysis of age and aging.

My daughters were grown and out of the house. By this time Peggy had begun her career as a top hospital administrator. She got these positions despite her last name, Foner, which was very familiar to hospital personnel directors. Nancy, an anthropologist teaching at the State University of New York at Purchase, had done research in the Caribbean and would go on to be an expert on immigration to New York. One of her books was a study of health care workers in a New York nursing home, which was not at the time an 1199 facility. In 1982 I became a grandfather—to Alexis, the daughter of Nancy and her husband Peter Swerdloff.

Although my family was a very important part of my life, I felt a gap. I liked to swim, ride a bicycle, and play tennis; I read a lot, especially political biographies and books about the media; and I socialized with friends, many of whom went back to my student days in the 1930s. But I felt these were things to enjoy *after* work. I had always worked long hours, and unless I had a project I was excited about, I felt something was missing. Plus I felt the union I loved and helped to build was destroying itself.

That self-destruction came to a head in the 1984 strike. Acting unilaterally, without consulting her Executive Council, Turner called a strike of fifty thousand workers at forty-one hospitals on July 13, 1984. The strike lasted until August 27 and was by almost everyone's accounts one of the most inept, unplanned, and disastrous strikes in New York history.

Workers walked out without clear goals. They had no picket signs, strike committees, or union support of any kind. Turner chose to strike on a Friday, which meant workers would lose two days pay over the weekend when the hospital censuses were low and the strike would have little effect on management. Picket lines were pitifully weak. But while strikers searched for support and leadership, Turner and her lieutenants shared expensive suites, meals, and champagne at the Roosevelt Hotel.

Until the strike, Exec. Vice Pres. David White, an African-American former licensed practical nurse with a long history of political and union activism, had supported Turner as a matter of racial unity. But when he saw the officers partying in luxury while strikers suffered on the sidewalks below he became physically sick and handed in his resignation. White's defection became very important later.

Pressure mounted for a settlement, and at a Madison Square Garden rally August 27, Turner announced triumphantly that she'd won two annual 5 percent raises with no givebacks. The members enthusiastically voted to approve the settlement, not knowing that Turner had lied to them. The agreement did contain givebacks in benefits, and because Turner blocked their implementation, management withheld the second 5 percent raise.

The missing 5 percent became a central issue when an anti-Turner group called Save Our Union (SOU) mounted an opposition campaign aimed at the 1986 union elections. I supported SOU in any way I could.

Another main election issue was made possible by David White. Soon after the strike, I was talking with labor historian Leon Fink. Fink and his fellow historian Brian Greenberg were working on a history of 1199, which was published by the University of Illinois Press in 1989 under the title *Upheaval in the Quiet Zone*. It's an excellent book, a thorough and balanced study unlike many union histories that are just puff pieces. *Upheaval* is mandatory reading for those interested in 1199, although in the interest of full disclosure I must add that I helped get the project started and underwritten. In their introduction, Fink and Greenberg call me the book's "patient godfather."

As part of his research, Fink had interviewed White. On a fall day in 1984, shortly after interviewing White, Fink took me into my office and closed the door.

"Somebody should talk to David White. I can't say anything more than that, but it's very important for you," Fink said.

I talked to one of SOU's top leaders, Dennis Rivera. Rivera had come to New York in 1977 from Puerto Rico, where he was a student activist and union organizer. He quickly joined the 1199 staff as an organizer. Dennis was a Davis supporter, and when Turner fired him he preserved his 1199 membership by working as a messenger at Beth Israel Hospital until Turner got them to illegally fire him. (The firing was later overturned.) Then he went to work at United Presbyterian Residence on Long Island. He was in his early thirties back then, a tireless worker for SOU with a lot of energy and ideas.

Rivera talked to David White. He called me back and shouted, "Moe, we've got it now!"

After his resignation, a deeply disillusioned White had gone to the Department of Labor and filed an affidavit charging massive vote tampering in Turner's reelection as president in the spring of 1984. What he described to Rivera in detail was this: He and a dozen other Turner loyalists had worked through that April 1984 night at union headquarters where paper ballots were stored awaiting official counting. The Turner people threw out several large black plastic garbage bags full of Slate 2 (anti-Turner) ballots and substituted ballots filled in by the staff for Slate 1 (the Turner ticket). This was later corroborated by three other staffers who were there with White.

"We've got to go public," I said to Rivera. "And before that, I want David White to read that statement into a tape recorder." Then, remembering that SOU was operating on a shoestring, I added, "Make sure it's a tape recorder that works."

Rivera taped White. The tape recorder worked and the tape was dynamite. I called White to make sure he was willing to go public.

"I'm prepared to do anything. I'm ready to die," he said.

That wasn't just dramatics. White told me there were five or six people around Turner all the time, ex-prisoners with guns who played for keeps. Going public could be dangerous.

We made copies of the statement and drafted a press release. Then I had a sound technician friend make five hundred copies of White's recording. We called them the "Turnergate Tapes," and, after we broke the news, we sold the tapes to members to help finance SOU.

I took White's story to the press selectively, calling different reporters and getting the most mileage possible. The *Post* broke it first. Then the *Times* labor reporter, Bill Serrin, did a long and thorough article in which Turner refused to comment. Joe Conason had a piece in the *Village Voice*, and the *Amsterdam News*, *City Sun* (a black-owned weekly in Brooklyn), and *El Diario* ran with the story for weeks. Television and radio picked it up. TV reporters stood outside 1199 headquarters saying, "Doris Turner is not available for comment." Finally, early in 1985, Gil Noble interviewed Turner and White separately on his ABC-TV show *Like It Is*. Turner did a lot of character assassination on White, but she wasn't able to turn the tide. Her credibility was seriously shaken.

The core group at SOU included former Vice Pres. Kay, a former drugstore clerk who was SOU's highest-ranking ousted 1199 officer; Rivera; a fired organizer, Marshall Garcia; National Union Exec. Vice Pres. Bob Muehlenkamp; Georgianna Johnson, who was a social work aide at Hospital for Joint Diseases in Harlem; and me. Bill Lynch, a political consultant who was later a deputy mayor under Mayor David Dinkins, was our close advisor. We'd call him all the time.

Every Wednesday night fifty or sixty SOU people would meet at SOU headquarters in the West 80s in Manhattan to discuss and approve plans. The approval process became a big problem for me. I wasn't used to checking what I was going to say to the press in advance with a dozen people. Eventually I got the freedom I needed, and it worked well. Rivera handled the *Amsterdam News, City Sun,* and *El Diario,* and I handled the rest. I called him every morning around seven o'clock to check the angle for the day and how we'd play it. We did the same thing with political moves.

Our focus was on the 1986 election. You can't beat somebody with nobody, and we knew that to beat Turner our somebody had to be a black woman. Georgianna Johnson was the logical choice. She wasn't charismatic like Turner and she wasn't widely known to the members, but she was committed and hard-working, and she was a quietly effective campaigner in the hospitals. Johnson headed a balanced SOU slate for top officer positions that included six blacks, four Hispanics, and three non-Hispanic whites. Almost half were rank-and-file members.

The Department of Labor required Turner to hand over the membership mailing list to opposing candidates, but she delayed so long that we had to use first-class mail, which is expensive. Still, we did three mailings, including a four-page newspaper. Raising money was an enormous problem. Members contributed a lot. We had raffles. We had frequent dances, some raising as much as ten thousand dollars. Using direct mail to about five hundred people, I personally raised more than thirty thousand dollars. Direct-mail experts tell me that kind of return is very unusual. Eventually we raised more than $100,000 for the campaign.

Leon Davis wasn't well, but he'd come up from retirement in Florida to campaign in hospitals. To counter the charge that SOU was racist, we got endorsements from Ossie Davis, Ruby Dee, and Paul Robeson, Jr.

Our main theme was the missing 5 percent raise. But there were other issues. Turner's administration was chaotic. A thousand unresolved grievances had piled up. Members were being laid off. The impression was spreading that the union was incapable of dealing with management.

Still, it's hard to dislodge incumbent union leaderships. Turner had a hundred staff people to use as campaign workers. She had uninterrupted access to the members. She had considerable management support, which meant that SOU campaigners were kept outside the institutions. She had lots of money. She used the local's publication as a puff sheet. Each issue before the election had fifteen to twenty-five pictures of her. Also, she was able to manipulate the voting to her advantage. Members who worked in hospitals on Long Island where there was known Turner opposition had to travel as far as fifty miles to vote, while at the smallest pro-Turner institutions, members voted inside. In addition, AFL-CIO Pres. Lane Kirkland and RWDSU Pres. Al Heaps were publicly supporting Turner. They supplied legal and public relations help.

Once again, we realized we needed to reach members through the media. After the initial coverage of David White's revelations, momentum was slowing. One of Rivera's jobs was to talk directly to the members through the hotline at WBLS, the black radio station. We got occasional stuff in the *Voice, Amsterdam News,* and *City Sun,* and persuaded the *Amsterdam* not to endorse Turner as it had in 1984.

But the daily papers were harder. Their interest in labor news has declined considerably in recent decades. Still, after a while I got *Newsday* and the *Daily News* to use stories and op-ed pieces, and as soon as they appeared we'd have them photocopied and distributed in the hospitals within hours. Then the *News* and the *Times* got involved editorially, coming close to endorsing Georgianna Johnson.

As the election in April approached, we knew we had a shot at winning. We had 150 rank-and-file members trained as organizers and covering the hospitals. One of the turning points came when Ossie Davis addressed a pre-election SOU conference at Columbia University. Ossie read a telegram from the RWDSU's president warning him not to get involved. Then he delivered a speech saying why he had to be involved in the effort to get 1199 back on the right track. He recalled his long association with us, the many 1199 picket lines he and his family had walked, and the principled positions he shared with our union. He spoke of the meaning 1199 had always provided in his life.

Dennis Rivera called me and said, "I've never heard anything so moving. People walked out crying!"

We made three hundred tapes of Ossie's speech and distributed them to members. Ossie also made time in a particularly busy schedule to work with Johnson, preparing her for a debate with Turner scheduled for Gil Noble's *Like It Is* show on ABC-TV. But Turner backed out and the debate never happened.

The Department of Labor ran the election, with balloting extending over ten days. The final tally was 18,972 for Johnson and 16,039 for Turner. But we weren't out of the woods yet.

The AFL-CIO had backed Turner. It had a lot of influence on the Department of Labor. What if they prevailed on the Department to "investigate" the results and delay seating the victorious SOU?

Dennis went to Washington to lobby for congressional pressure to seat the winners promptly. He called me and said, "I shouldn't ask you this. But the people here say something on the opinion pages of the *Times* would be fantastic." When the op-ed piece we needed appeared the following Monday he called and said, "Moe, you're a genius." What he didn't know was that my eagerness to get the piece published almost killed it.

I'd been working to get a piece favorable to SOU in the *Times* editorial page for weeks. Finally, editorial board member and former *Times* labor reporter A. H. (Abe) Raskin looked over our material and agreed to do an op-ed piece. But a couple of weeks went by and nothing appeared. I was friendly with *Times* reporter Joan Cook, whose husband Gerry had worked at *1199 News*. I called her and asked how we could speed things up.

"I'll walk over and talk to the assistant op-ed editor," said Cook, and she mentioned his name.

Nothing appeared for another week, so I called the assistant editor myself. His response was very cold.

"That is a matter between the *Times* and Abe Raskin. You are irrelevant," he said.

"Look," I said. "I apologize. Would you make believe I never called you?"

I called Cook. She was horrified.

"What have you done?" she said. "That's a big no-no."

But the piece did appear, just in time. Soon afterward, SOU was seated. The night before SOU was scheduled to move back into 1199 headquarters at 310 West 43rd Street in Manhattan, we had a big party. People kept coming in to report how all day long, trucks pulled up to the headquarters and Turner's people took stuff out of the building. Among the union property that vanished were a wonderful painting of Frederick Douglass by Charles White and a precious political action poster set Ben Shahn had done for the CIO forty years earlier. Also presumed missing were any documents that would have been incriminating if then-U.S. Attorney Rudolph Giuliani had continued his grand jury investigation of the Turner presidency.

But for us, as we celebrated the Save Our Union victory, it was like a candle that had gone out was lit again.

8. Senior Advisor

Passing It On

THE SAVE Our Union victory in 1986 did not immediately fix the busted violin that Dave Livingston said 1199 had become. But it turned us in the right direction. That direction has led us to our current position of greater size and power than most of us dreamed of back then. Still, fixing the magnificent instrument that 1199 had once been took time.

The three-year presidency of Georgianna Johnson was difficult. Her term ended bitterly, with Doris Turner supporting Johnson against Dennis Rivera in the union's 1989 election of officers. Rivera won the presidency with an overwhelming majority, but the whole affair had disturbing overtones. Johnson was, after all, the second black woman in three years to be voted out of office. Like Turner, she left feeling she was a victim of white men. How did that happen?

I was removed from the day-to-day running of 1199, and I have only a hazy idea of the details. I know that the initial plan was for team leadership in which Johnson would work together with more experienced leaders like Eddie Kay.

Union leaders tend to be aggressive types whose intensity level in dealing with the employer is not always lowered at union headquarters. Kay was a veteran 1199 officer with an impressive record in building a powerful 1199 rank-and-file organization on Long Island. But he may not have been the easiest person for Johnson to work with. She felt he and others excluded her from decision making.

People used to say the same thing about Davis, Jesse Olson (head of 1199's Guild of Technical, Professional, Office and Clerical Employees), and me. We all lived in the same part of Queens and often drove to work together. Turner would angrily say we made all the important decisions in the car every morning, leaving her out.

Did we? It's true that we talked about union business in the car. Union business consumed us. We talked about it all the time. And because we had similar political backgrounds, we understood each other without detailed explanations. We trusted each other's commitment and ability. So it was natural for us to make plans in the car.

But Dave was always careful to broaden policy discussions to include all the officers and eventually the delegates and the members. He never acted until he felt he had consensus expressed by a democratic vote.

I suspect the people around Georgianna Johnson acted in the same way. She was inexperienced, and I can certainly imagine that at times other officers acted without consulting her. I've been told that when she felt excluded she made matters worse by withdrawing almost completely from the union's leadership.

I don't pretend to have all the answers to the questions about 1199 raised by the troubles of the 1980s. To some extent we all played out events based on our backgrounds, and mistakes were made. But the union survived.

ONE of the first things the union did after SOU took office was to organize home care workers. Home care was a fast-growing field in which minority women, most of them from other countries, were terribly exploited—as they remain today.

Home care workers in the 1980s were ignored by the labor movement, just as hospital workers had been thirty years earlier. Working in the mid-1980s with AFSCME Local 1707, we quickly organized about thirty thousand home care workers. The problem was getting enough public attention to force the state funding that would make a decent contract possible. First, we persuaded David Dinkins, Manhattan's borough president, to hold public hearings in which the workers themselves could describe their miserable conditions.

Then, in 1987, we did a big media campaign. *Newsday* ran a week-long series of front-page stories, starting with "Home Care Workers: The Shame of New York City."

I was calling around to the media as I had in 1959. After all we had gone through, it felt good to be able to work again in a clear-cut crusade for justice. While I wasn't a union officer, I was in the office to work at Bread and Roses, and I functioned as kind of a senior advisor to people like Dennis Rivera. Dennis and I had formed a close friendship during the SOU campaign, and after the 1986 victory we continued our pattern of almost daily early-morning telephone conversations.

The home care campaign picked up steam. We had street rallies in lower Manhattan of ten thousand home care workers. We formed an alliance with the Reverend James Forbes of Riverside Church and had huge rallies there. We published a powerful series of paintings in *1199 News* on a day in the life of a home care worker by Robert Felker, a student I recruited through the dean of the School of Visual Arts, Marshall Arisman.

Then I suggested to Rivera that we approach Cardinal John O'Connor, Roman Catholic archbishop of New York, who was decidedly pro-labor, and ask for his support. Dennis did, and we had an unusual press conference on the steps of St. Patrick's Cathedral in which the Cardinal, Rev. Jesse Jackson, and Rivera spoke out for home care workers.

The result of all this was improved pay and benefits, although home care workers still are exploited and much remains to be done. 1199 was moving, and the 1989 expiration of our big contract with the League of Voluntary Hospitals was approaching.

The 1989 contract campaign signaled to the world that 1199 was back. Through a masterfully orchestrated series of short strikes and massive marches, the union won major wage and benefit gains.

This was especially remarkable coming only five years after the disastrous Turner-led strike of 1984. Members wanted to catch up after nearly a decade of mediocre contracts, but it would have been impossible to get them to go out again in an open-ended strike. Rivera started cautiously, with a one-day strike and march July 11 starting in Central Park. The turnout of thirty-five thousand members floored everybody.

Our campaign picked up momentum, and soon 1199ers seemed to be marching and rallying everywhere. Some thirty-five thousand members led by Rivera and Jackson marched through upper Manhattan from St. Luke's Hospital to Mount Sinai Hospital July 24. On August 10, four thousand members marched up Manhattan's East Side from Beth Israel Hospital to a candlelight vigil at New York University Medical Center. In between were rallies at Riverside Church and elsewhere. During a three-day mid-August strike, forty thousand members rallied at Battery Park in lower Manhattan August 14, twenty-five thousand members marched from Montefiore Hospital to Beth Abraham nursing home in the Bronx August 15, and many thousands of members demonstrated August 16 outside of fifty-three struck institutions.

Early in the campaign, Rivera skillfully arranged a separate contract with Cardinal O'Connor. In it, the Catholic hospitals agreed to a pattern of wage and benefit improvements that eventually was adopted citywide in a settlement reached on the eve of an October 4 union deadline for a full-scale strike.

The spectacle of a contract victory by a fighting union that could mobilize massive numbers of members showed everybody that 1199 was once again alive and healthy.

I was on the sidelines during this campaign, having hip replacement surgery. While recuperating at home, I'd talk with Dennis and make press calls to place stories. I helped out with concepts, including demonstration slogans directed at management such as "Do the Right Thing" and "Thou Shalt Not Steal." The latter was a reference to the missing 5 percent raise, which we eventually got.

DURING the late 1980s, I was also involved in the merger campaign of the National Union. The National Union, minus 1199 in New York, which remained in the Retail, Wholesale and Department Store Union (RWDSU), received a separate independent charter from the AFL-CIO as part of the 1984 merger dispute settlement. But with only seventy-five thousand members in a dozen districts across the country, the National Union was spread too thin. All its leaders wanted to merge with a larger international, but some wanted to go with the Service Employees International Union (SEIU) and some wanted to go with the American Federation of State, County and Municipal Employees (AFSCME).

I still thought SEIU was the best fit because its members, like ours, were in the private sector. I worked as an informal advisor to the leaders of the pro-SEIU faction. They were National Union Sec. Treas. Jerry Brown, who was head of the big New England district, and Exec. Vice Pres. Bob Muehlenkamp, who was director of organizing. National Union Pres. Henry Nicholas, my old partner in the Charleston strike, headed the AFSCME faction.

The dispute proved irreconcilable, and in 1989 members in each National Union district voted to merge their district with either SEIU or AFSCME. Districts including two thirds of the members chose SEIU. One third went to AFSCME.

The result was confusing. Today, locals like 1199C in Philadelphia and 1199J in New Jersey belong to AFSCME, while 1199/New England, 1199P in Pennsylvania outside Philadelphia, 1199E in Maryland and Washington, D.C., and 1199NW in Washington State belong to SEIU.

1199 in New York withdrew from the RWDSU in 1991 and joined SEIU in 1998. The SEIU connection provided immediate benefits. The SEIU has 1.3 million members and is now the second largest AFL-CIO union. Its 350,000–member New York State Council, now headed by Dennis Rivera, gives 1199 tremendous political influence. With SEIU help in organizing, 1199 has doubled in size and now has 210,000 members.

For me, 1199's affiliation with SEIU was a great event. I'd been for it ever since 1959 when I met with leaders of SEIU's Local 250, which does a good job representing hospital workers in San Francisco. Davis and I met with SEIU Pres. George Hardy in the late 1970s, when merger talks started in earnest. It's taken a long time, but Davis's dream of one big union for all health care workers is now much closer to reality.

THE Dennis Rivera who took office as 1199 president in 1989 was an impressive young man of thirty-eight who had come to New

York from Puerto Rico twelve years earlier. My first encounter with him was in the late 1970s. He came to my office and asked for authorization to hire a bus to take Hispanic members to a demonstration the following day in Washington, D.C. I forget the subject of the demonstration, but I remember being angry.

"You can't come to me this late," I told him. "I don't have time to take it to the Executive Council for approval. Next time, plan ahead."

He left disappointed, but, as I mentioned above, we later became close during the SOU campaign. I began to realize during the campaign that Dennis is an unusual person. He's charming and graceful, but beneath the "if you please" and "I'd appreciate it if you could," he's very determined. He's also extremely smart and a quick learner.

He's like Davis in a number of ways. Rivera is also totally committed to the interests of the members and to their involvement in union activities. And like Davis, he's an immigrant with an accent. It's interesting how the two men handled that. Dave was self-conscious about his Russian accent and let others, like me, speak for the union. Dennis, on the other hand, doesn't let his slight Spanish accent stop him for a minute. He's persuasive with the press and with political leaders.

I decided that after the decade of bad publicity we'd had, it would be a good idea to project this attractive new leader. I asked Abe Raskin about a profile in the Sunday *Times Magazine*. The *Times* didn't go for it, but the *New Yorker* magazine did. Rivera agreed, although it meant having Raskin follow him everywhere for several months. Raskin attended all the union meetings, sat around in Dennis's office, and even went to Puerto Rico to interview Dennis's family and friends. The article, titled "Getting Things Done," appeared December 10, 1990. It was the most detailed description of Dennis that's ever appeared. It was also the first profile of a labor leader the *New Yorker* had done since it profiled A. Philip Randolph in 1973.

Raskin suffered a serious stroke when the piece was in the proofreading stage. He could read, but he couldn't speak. His wife called and asked me to come over.

"Abe keeps pointing to something in the copy, but I can't understand what he wants," she said.

I went with misgivings, because I knew newspaper people don't like to show their stories in advance to the people involved.

"I know this is irregular, but if you let me look the story over I'll make corrections and you can nod if you agree," I told Raskin.

He agreed and that's how we did it. Of course, I only changed typos and minor errors of fact.

After the *New Yorker* piece appeared, I kept after the *Times*. I finally interested urban affairs columnist Sam Roberts, and his profile of Dennis appeared in the May 10, 1992, Sunday *Times Magazine*, which has a circulation of two million. The magazine had a photo of Dennis's face on the cover. The headline read, "A New Face for American Labor." The article said, "Dennis Rivera has become a forceful presence in New York and a power in Hispanic politics nationally."

The *Times* and *New Yorker* profiles stressed Dennis's energy, his skill in dealing with members and employers, and his early successes in healing the union's internal wounds. Such widely read publicity helped restore some of our positive image, and because of 1199's achievements in the past decade and Dennis's skill in presenting them to the media, I think that image has remained positive.

LEON Davis died September 14, 1992, at the age of eighty-four. Everyone wanted a memorial, and they all agreed when I suggested it should be at Avery Fisher Hall in Lincoln Center. I approached George Weissman, a college friend who had become president of the Lincoln Center board, and he arranged for us to rent the hall for October 5. We filled it with twenty-eight hundred people for a program that I organized and emceed. The speakers included Rivera, Mayor David Dinkins, Coretta King, Ossie Davis, Ruby Dee, retired Mount Sinai nurse's aide and 1959 strike veteran Josephine Bell, and Davis's daughter, Liane Vida Davis, representing Davis's wife Julia and the rest of the Davis family.

Another speaker was Dr. Martin Cherkasky, who headed Montefiore in 1958 when it became the first hospital to vote 1199 in. Davis and Cherkasky had remained friendly ever since. I was glad that only a few weeks earlier I had taken Cherkasky and Dennis Rivera to visit Dave at his home in Queens.

Perhaps Davis's character was best summed up at the memorial by 1199/New England Pres. Jerry Brown:

> Dave disdained money, personal prestige, comfort, or political power unless it was in service of the union. He was single-minded, irascible, angry, impatient, and impossible. But he was a hero. After his anger over poverty, war, and exploitation, there was hope and a dream of a better world of racial unity and workers' power. And that dream lives on in 1199 all over the country.

One of the speakers at the Davis memorial was a union activist who had been a cantor. I'd asked him just to chant the Jewish prayer for the dead. He did that, and did it well. But then he followed the prayer with an attack on the new union leadership, which was totally inappropriate in that setting. I was boiling mad, but I couldn't get him to stop.

After the event we had a short gathering at union headquarters. I was still agitated, and as I left I passed out. An ambulance took me to St. Clare's Hospital, where I stayed for about a week. It turned out that I have a heart condition. That condition became more serious in 1998, when I could no longer do my part in caring for our house in Queens. Anne and I moved to an apartment on the Upper West Side of Manhattan. Soon after that I was hospitalized for nearly four months. Since then, I've been confined mostly to home. There have been various setbacks, but I exercise as much as I can to regain my strength, maintain a careful diet, and stay busy. Esther Cohen of Bread and Roses and other union people visit regularly to discuss work, and I practically live on the phone.

I'M fortunate that my younger daughter, Peggy, lives in our apartment building and my older daughter Nancy and her family live nearby. I get to see them regularly, and I'm grateful for that. While the major burden for my care falls on Anne, Nancy and Peggy have been supportive and attentive. In a way there's been a reversal of roles since my illness. I looked after my daughters to the best of my ability when they were little. Later on, I was the anxious parent concerned about their getting into college, their health, their first jobs. Now they look after me.

The story I've told here may present me as so obsessed with my work that family was just background. That isn't true. Family is very important to me. In my early years I tried to be a good son and brother. Later, I took being a husband and father just as seriously. While I wish I had been around my family more when my daughters were little, being a parent and a husband has been a wonderful part of my life. Anne, who has been my wife for nearly sixty years now, reminds me that while I may not have been a feminist, I definitely helped in running our household. That included washing dishes, making beds, vacuuming, shopping for food on Saturday mornings, and so on.

Nancy and Peggy maintain that despite my long hours at work I did my best to carry on in the "anything for the children" tradition that I grew up with. When they were little, I ferried them around to friends, music lessons, and school. When they were in summer camp, I wrote them long letters every day, with a stick of gum enclosed. Anne and I never missed a camp visiting day—and I've even carried on that tradition by visiting our granddaughter—Nancy's daughter Alexis—when she's been at summer camp. Wherever Nancy and Peggy were, we visited them, and that's provided some of my fondest travel memories. We visited Nancy in England during her junior year abroad and later for a week in rural Jamaica when she was doing fieldwork as part of her anthropology career. I still remember the goats braying there at four in the morning. We accompanied Peggy when she revisited the college in Yorkshire, England, where she had spent a year abroad. We met her English friends there and enjoyed their visits when they came to the United States.

Summers and holidays have remained important family times, and we still get together often. When our daughters were small, we took them on vacations before and after camp. When Nancy and Peggy were older, we'd spend summer vacations at Anne's parents' house in Hampton Bays, Long Island, and they'd bring their teenaged and college friends.

In addition to our children, Anne and I have enjoyed a tight circle of friends we've known for sixty years and more and still see regularly. Some of our social life also grew out of friendships I made at 1199. Leon Davis and his wife Julia lived near us in Queens, and every New Year's Day we'd go to their annual party, for instance. In the summer they'd have us over for barbecues.

Just as I feel lucky to have been in the right place at the right time to participate in many key public events of our era, I feel fortunate in my private life. I'm surrounded by my family, I still have my work, and I feel I have a lot more to achieve through the new projects of Bread and Roses. What more could a man ask?

In my role as an advisor from the sidelines, I sometimes get asked general questions by people who want to work in public relations, labor journalism, or union cultural programs. Here are some of my thoughts on how to succeed in these areas.

Public relations sometimes gets a bum rap. The image is of slick hired guns who say anything for money. While this is often the reality, too many unions use this negative image to justify doing nothing to present their case to the public.

There's no getting around the fact that public opinion is important, especially to a union like ours that depends so much on political decisions. And there's also no getting around the fact that if you don't try to get your story to the public, your enemies will, and it won't be pretty.

So I believe in effective union public relations. These are some of the principles I developed through trial and error:

First of all, answer phone calls. Too many unions still try to hide from the media. That always hurts you in the long run. It's better to get to know the reporters, their needs, their personalities, their deadlines, and so on. Then you have an opportunity to present your case rather than have the other side frame the issues.

You have to develop skills in reaching the right people. Some of that is just a lot of hard work, a lot of phone calls. Going through this person to reach that person. Usually nowadays this is done by big public relations firms. But I worked by myself. I remember when we finally won the 1962 legislative campaign in Albany to get col-

lective bargaining rights for hospital workers, Governor Rockefeller's counsel came up to me and said:

"Moe, you must have spent an enormous amount of money on
this campaign. Which Madison Ave. firm handled it?"

"You're looking at him right now," I said.

"You must be kidding," he answered.

But it was true.

Besides hard work, if you want to be successful in this field you
have to respect reporters. You have to be sure that the facts you give
them are accurate. They have to trust you. If you make things up or
lie to them, you're dead. They'll know you're a conniver.

Also, they have to feel that you're committed to the cause you're
talking about.

And finally, be persistent. In my case they knew if they didn't answer my call, I would keep calling; they'd never hear the end of it.
You have to be a nudge. You have to keep pestering. I remember
hearing Marian Wright Edelman, president of the Children's Defense Fund, say, "We need pests for good things." I agree with her.

Sometimes I reached the point where I'd say, "Gee, I'm embar-
rassed. Should I call?" But usually I would. And people would get
the attitude, "If I don't do what he wants, he'll never go away."

Eventually, I realized that a lot of people of good conscience felt
we were actually doing them a favor by enlisting their aid. They
wanted to be part of an effective organization working for social
justice, and they were glad to find us.

In this regard, maintaining the right reputation was essential. We
came to be identified with good causes—the civil rights movement,
opposition to the war in Vietnam, support for peace and nuclear
disarmament. When Cesar Chavez came to New York looking for
support in the early days of the United Farm Workers, he had a
nickel and Leon Davis's phone number in his pocket. Some people
began to use us as a yardstick. They'd think, "If 1199 is for it, then
it must be good."

They might not be fond of unions in general, but we'd seem like a
breath of fresh air. Having that kind of good name is very important. Because it also means when we needed help, there were people
to turn to. With a network like that, it's a two-way street. I had to

think about positions we took. We didn't want to embarrass our allies. We couldn't identify with every campaign in the world.

Some people say that 1199 over the years has relied too much on the public arena—politics and public relations—and not enough on the organized strength of our members. My experience is that you have to have both. An effective union functions on many levels. To win any struggle, the members have to be committed and involved. The staff has to do its job. The leadership has to have vision and dedication. And someone has to be able to get the union story out and win allies and political support.

That last part is especially important in an industry like ours, which relies so heavily on government funding. But I could talk myself blue in the face, and if the rest of the pieces weren't in place, no one would listen to me. And even if you can place stories once in a while, if your union is an empty shell, nothing will come of it.

I was in charge of communications at 1199 for thirty years. Besides public relations and internal union communication, that meant I supervised the union's monthly magazine, *1199 News*. Our magazine has for many decades been regarded as one of the labor movement's top publications. I think several principles contribute to this. My sense is that these principles apply to any kind of union communication, including leaflets, brochures, videos, websites, and so on.

Consider the visual. Union members get their publication in the mail. They don't make a decision to buy it, it just arrives in the house. They have to make a quick decision about whether to look at it or throw it out. So it's important for the publication to be attractive enough to catch and maintain their attention. That means paying for good paper, good printing, good designers, and good photos. Not many labor papers have staff photographers, but we hired one of the best, Jim Tynan, in 1992 after I saw his work at a gallery in Soho. He's been a tremendous asset to *1199 News*. Stanley Glaubach designed the magazine for many years. When he died, his wife, Marjorie, a skilled artist who had worked with Stan since their student days at Cooper Union, came on staff full-time as art director of *1199 News* and carried on in his tradition of graphic excellence.

And I've been helped consistently over the years by the advice of people such as Pam Vassil, a top designer in the magazine and academic world.

Then there's the writing. I found that it can't be philosophical. It should be simple and clear. I tried to avoid insider's jargon that assumes members know things they may not know. And it has to be about something that members feel affects their lives. Even if it's a national or international issue, it has to start with some local angle. It takes talented people to do this, and over the years we've had many skilled and committed writers and editors.

A union publication is a house organ, but it shouldn't be outrageously self-serving. It should observe basic standards of journalistic integrity. Its job is to educate, unite, and mobilize members. For this to happen, the member has to feel the publication is trustworthy. It can't lie, it has to get the relevant facts right, and I believe it has to provide some degree of balance.

To avoid building a cult of personality, I insisted on one thing: that Davis's picture should appear with his column and never anyplace else, unless it was some kind of sensational event. Jimmy Wechsler, the editor of the *New York Post* (which was an entirely different newspaper before Rupert Murdoch became its publisher), and I used to be on the phone all the time. We would each get *The Pilot*, which was the paper of the National Maritime Union (NMU), and we'd count the number of pictures of NMU Pres. Joe Curran. Then we'd call each other.

"I got seventeen," I'd say.

"You're wrong. I got eighteen," he'd answer.

Some union leaders use their publications for self-promotion all the time. Whenever I see this I assume the publication is of little value. Members have to be treated with respect. If they see their president all over the publication, they understand that the union is just about reelecting the incumbent leaders. But if they see, as is the case at *1199 News*, that instead of stories about officers there are interviews and pictures of workers on the job and in their homes, they understand that the publication—and by implication the union—is about the members.

Another thing I encouraged in our magazine was debate and differences of opinion, particularly through letters to the editor. Many editors throw letters that criticize the leadership into the wastebasket. They may be acting on instructions from leaders who fear dissent or they may be their own censors. Most of the time I had the green light to print critical letters, and I did. I think it created trust among members that their views meant something.

IN the area of cultural programs, you need several things to succeed. You need a passionate commitment to bring the best there is to working people. You need to listen to representative, articulate members of the union and stay aware of what kind of programs they want. And you need a sense of integrity.

When you have a high-visibility program like Bread and Roses, there are pressures for censorship. For example, we had people on the union staff who objected to paintings of nudes in Gallery 1199. They said members would be offended. But we did it anyway, and no members complained.

Another kind of pressure comes when you accept money or help from outside the union. Donors sometimes want strings attached. Or just the nature of a potential donor can be a problem. For instance, we don't accept money from tobacco or alcohol companies.

A few years ago we organized New York high school students to take pictures of anything that interested them in Times Square. The goal was a photo exhibit. The 42nd Street Development Corporation, a private agency that has helped clean up the area, worked with us on the project.

We held regular meetings with the students and their teachers to go over their photos. The Development Corporation people came to one of the meetings. They loved what they saw until they came to a photo that showed a derelict.

"You can't have that," said their executive director. "It won't help what we're doing."

The Development Corporation was prepared to display and advertise our photos all over Times Square and in the subways, said the executive director. But not if we insisted on including the picture of a homeless person.

"Would you excuse yourself for a few minutes?" I asked.

We discussed the problem. My position was that we couldn't accept that kind of censorship. The students, teachers, and Bread and Roses staff all agreed. It was unanimous. So we lost the Development Corporation's help but kept our integrity.

I think the students felt good about it. They learned that we stand for something and there are certain things we won't do, even if it means losing money and visibility. I mean, what kind of a lesson would it be to the student who took that picture if we excluded it? She saw the homeless person with her own eyes, and banishing her photo would be like telling her that money is more important than reality.

I'M very lucky. I was in the right place at the right time, and I became part of something good and important. I'm proud that the Davis generation I was a part of built a lasting legacy for 1199 and for whomever else wants to look at the record.

That legacy is commitment and concern for the members of our union and for working people in general. Through the last seventy years, the leadership of 1199 was prepared to walk through fire to get what was just and right for workers.

Nobody dreamed four decades ago that we could organize hospital workers. People asked, "Why are you doing this? It's crazy."

"We're doing this because it's a problem we can't ignore," answered Davis and the people around him.

That thread runs throughout our history. I'm proud that I worked in a union where the president said to me, "Yes, spend as much time as you can to develop a labor focus on the Vietnam War," and that he said the same thing about the civil rights movement, disarmament, and other broad issues.

Our ability to make an impact is so much greater today. We're part of the SEIU, which has well over a million members. We lead the SEIU's New York State Council, which has 350,000 members.

We have 210,000 members ourselves. And President Dennis Rivera is supremely skilled in making politics work for working people.

I never wanted more than I had at 1199. I was proud of our low salary scale for staff and officers. I never wanted to be the richest or most important person in the world. I just feel lucky I've had the opportunity to do what I've done. Who would have guessed back when I was playing schoolyard basketball in Williamsburg that I'd get a chance to work in a union that turned out to be like 1199?

For those who come after, I would urge a couple of things:

Get to understand and appreciate how and why this union was built, and stay close to those concepts. And stay close to the members. Do your best to serve them. If you do that, you'll be fine.

Epilogue

Moe Foner died January 10, 2002. At his funeral January 13, Ossie Davis, his friend of forty-eight years, said: "There was nothing left over in this man's life. Every bit of it was dedicated to the noble and the beautiful. And we're all the better for it." Many of Foner's friends and associates spoke April 24 at a "Celebrate MOE" tribute sponsored by 1199/SEIU at Town Hall in mid-Manhattan. The Bread and Roses Cultural Project begun by Foner in 1978 continues under the leadership of Executive Director Esther Cohen.

Dan North has worked in journalism since 1959. He worked on daily newspapers for six years and for 31 years edited *1199 News,* the monthly magazine of New York's largest health care union. He has been a high school teacher and a carpenter. He currently teaches journalism and media studies at the City University of New York.

Bibliography

For those who wish to learn more about 1199 and the organization of health care workers, here is a selected list of sources.

Books and Articles

Cahn, William. *Lawrence, 1912: The Bread and Roses Strike.* New York: Pilgrim Press, 1980.

Fink, Leon, and Brian Greenberg. *Upheaval in the Quiet Zone, A History of Hospital Workers' Union Local 1199.* Champaign, Ill.: University of Illinois Press, 1989.

Foner, Moe, "Beauty, Laughter, Song and Wisdom: My Life with the Bread and Roses Cultural Project." *Labor's Heritage,* Fall 2000/Winter 2001: 60–73.

Foner, Moe, ed. *Images of Labor.* New York: Pilgrim Press, 1981.

Foner, Philip S. *Organized Labor and the Black Worker, 1619–1973.* New York: Praeger, 1974. Chapters 23, 24.

Panetta, Leon E., and Peter Gall. *Bring Us Together: The Nixon Team and the Civil Rights Retreat.* Philadelphia: Lippincott, 1971. Chapter 12.

Pritchett, Wendell E., "A Northern Civil Rights Movement: Community Race Relations in Brooklyn and the Beth-El Hospital Strike of 1962." *Labor's Heritage,* Fall 1999/Winter 2000: 4–23.

Raskin, A. H. "Getting Things Done: A Profile of Dennis Rivera." *The New Yorker,* December 10, 1990.

Raskin, A. H. "A Union with Soul." *The New York Times Magazine,* March 22, 1970.

Roberts, Sam. "New Face for American Labor: Dennis Rivera." *The New York Times Magazine,* May 10, 1992.

Wakefield, Dan. "Hospital Workers Knock at the Door." *Dissent,* Winter 1959.

Wakefield, Dan. "Victims of Charity." *The Nation,* March 14, 1959.

Videotapes

1199: The History of a Fighting Union. Includes segments from several documentary films produced by 1199 over several decades.

I Am Somebody. A documentary on 1199's hospital strike in 1969 in Charleston, S.C.

On the Move: Victory for 1199. A documentary on the union's 1989 contract campaign.

Practical Dreamer: Leon Davis. A documentary produced when Davis retired in 1982. Narrated by Ossie Davis and Ruby Dee.

Audio Cassettes

Birth of 1199: The Early Years. Written by Ossie Davis. Dramatization with music of the organization of drugstore workers in the 1930s. Cast includes Ossie Davis, Ruby Dee, Will Geer, Gilbert Green, and John Randolph. Songs by Pete Seeger.

Information on how to purchase videos and cassettes is available from Bread and Roses Cultural Project, 330 West 42nd St., New York, NY 10036. Additional information is available through the Bread and Roses website: www.bread-and-roses.com.

Index